ADVANCED WRITING SKILLS

John Arnold & Jeremy Harmer

Longman

Longman Group UK Limited,
Longman House, Burnt Mill, Harlow,
Essex CM20 2JE, England
and Associated Companies throughout the world.

First published 1978
Eleventh impression 1988

Produced by Longman Group (FE) Ltd
Printed in Hong Kong

ISBN 0-582-55481-0

CONTENTS

ACKNOWLEDGEMENTS

We would like to thank the following people for their help and cooperation in the development of this book: the principal, teachers, and students of Eurocentre, Bournemouth for their help and encouragement; students at the Instituto Anglo-Mexicano in Mexico City; and the secretarial staff at Eurocentre, Bournemouth, in particular Heather Woodley and Mary Parsa. We would especially like to thank Jeff Stranks for his contribution, and Roger Scott for his help and advice.

John Arnold
Jeremy Harmer

FOREWORD

With this book, the tenth Eurocentre publication in our series *Teaching Languages to Adults*, we continue our programme of providing materials and techniques for language teaching in areas not yet fully covered.

The recent developments within the field of linguistics have shown a need for a new approach to teaching English at the Advanced level; with their experience as teachers in an organisation teaching adults, the authors have recognised the need to interpret such developments at a strictly practical level both for teachers and students.

Thus *Advanced Writing Skills* concentrates on the production of written English and incorporates new concepts of Advanced learning by leading the students from controlled use to free and individual production of appropriate language. In addition, this book provides the teacher with material suitable for a variety of learning situations.

It also offers many opportunities for really challenging and varied homework and encourages the responsible student to make full use of his self-study potential.

We believe – and the testing of the material in the English Eurocentres has proved it – that this book can make a valuable contribution to the teaching of English at the Advanced level for both teachers and students.

Erh. J. C. Waespi
Director of the foundation for
European Language and Educational Centres

GENERAL INTRODUCTION

In this book, language is treated under three headings

Functions   **Topic Notions**   **Grammar**

Under **Functions** we consider ways in which language is used, for example, *Giving Advice*. We then present some of the forms of language that can be used in performing such Functions, for example, *if you take my advice you will* ...
Under **Topic Notions** we deal with the vocabulary related to a particular subject or topic, for example, *Work*. Under **Grammar** we present and practise certain structural patterns.

THE COURSE

The course is designed for students who have either passed the Cambridge First Certificate examination or successfully completed an equivalent course of study.
By the end of this book, successful students will be able to use the Functions, Topic Notions, and Grammar studied to express themselves fluently and accurately, particularly in writing. Such students will be in a position to take the Cambridge Certificate of Proficiency examination after further training in the specific techniques necessary for that examination.

UNIT LAYOUT

Each unit contains

a) A Text, which exemplifies one or more Functional areas, and which is also about a particular topic, thus providing material for discussion and vocabulary extension.
b) Comprehension and Summary exercises.
c) Revision-Test (except Unit 1).
d) Presentation and practice of Functional Language.
e) Sentence construction (i.e. Grammar).
f) Features of Structure and Style occurring in the text.
g) Vocabulary extension.
h) Final Written Tasks, designed to integrate *(d)–(g)* above.

DESIGN

The course is designed in such a way that it can be used, at the one extreme, for intensive courses, and at the other, for private study. As many students at this level follow non-intensive courses they will find the private study potential of the book particularly valuable; a key is provided for the majority of the exercises. Thus, where timetabling makes this necessary, particular parts of the unit may be dealt with outside the classroom.
The following publications have been particularly useful in the preparation of this book

Leech and Svartvik, *A Communicative Grammar of English*, Longman, 1975.
Quirk and Greenbaum, *A University Grammar of English*, Longman, 1973.
Wilkins, *Linguistics in Language Teaching*, Edward Arnold, 1973.

INTRODUCTION TO STUDENTS

Read this, as it will help you to get the best out of the book.
This book is especially designed for students who have passed the Cambridge First Certificate examination or who have done a course to about the same level, and completed it successfully. This book will help you towards a higher level of English knowledge, and if you wish, towards the Cambridge Certificate of Proficiency examination.

THE LAYOUT OF EACH UNIT

Text designed to provide discussion material and show examples of the language you will be studying.

Exercises on the Text designed to test your ability to understand and take information out of the text and to give you practice in selecting particular points from the text and linking this information together within a limited number of words.

Revision-Test designed to give further practice in elements of language which you have already studied in previous units.

Functional Language provides opportunities to study and practise the language you need for particular purposes, such as SUGGESTING COURSES OF ACTION.

Sentence Construction this section revises and extends your grammatical knowledge of English.

Structure and Style provides opportunities to study and practise special stylistic features of written English.

Topic Vocabulary here you can learn words in groups which are all concerned with a particular topic.

Writing Tasks this is the main piece of practice in which you can use the language you have studied in the unit (as well as in previous units). These compositions have been chosen to represent the kinds of written tasks which you might one day want to perform in English.

THE RESOURCES FILE

At the back of the book you will find a section marked RESOURCES FILE. Here you will find pictures, forms, and other visual aids taken from newspapers and other sources. These aids are designed to give you extra practice and revision of what you have studied in the units.

IF YOU ARE FOLLOWING AN INTENSIVE COURSE (10 or more lessons a week), you can use this book under the guidance of your teacher(s). It is a good idea to read the passage of any unit in advance and look at the Talking Points section. There is a key to all of the exercises marked Ⓚ, so you can use the exercises for revision and extra practice as necessary.

IF YOU ARE FOLLOWING A NON-INTENSIVE COURSE (2–10 lessons a week), you will have to do the majority of the exercises on your own. There is a key provided for all the exercises where this is possible. If there are points in the explanations or exercises which you do not understand, ask your teachers about them when you have the opportunity.

You will have plenty of opportunities when using this book to talk about yourself, give your personal opinions, and say what *you* think. Remember that learning another language, especially at an advanced level, should be an opportunity to express yourself and your ideas clearly and fluently, and to enjoy learning to do this. We wish you every success in bringing your knowledge of English to an ADVANCED level.

TEACHER'S HANDLING NOTES

THE TEXT

It is suggested that students read the text to be worked on before coming to class.

EXERCISES ON THE TEXT

1 *Vocabulary*

This section is designed to show the students a variety of vocabulary in context. It should be done orally, preferably before the other exercises on the text.

2 *Talking Points*

These true/false questions are designed as oral classroom activity, e.g. the teacher reads the sentences and the students say whether the answer is true or false. The questions are not designed to focus on any particular aspect of language, but should form the basis for discussion on the subject-matter of the text.

3 *Writing Points*

These questions could be done orally, but the intention is that the student should be able to write *complete* answers, as he will have to do in the Proficiency examination.

4 *Context Questions*

These questions could be dealt with either orally, or in writing. They are designed to test the student's in-depth understanding of the text.

5 *Summary Work*

The main aim of this is to train students to summarise, within given word limits, information they have read. The exercises can be used successfully as group work in the class.

REVISION-TEST

These can be done most effectively in the classroom under quasi-test conditions. The very act of doing the test should reinforce students' ability to use the language which they have studied and help them to commit that language to their memories.

FUNCTIONAL LANGUAGE, SENTENCE CONSTRUCTION, STRUCTURE AND STYLE

Since these various aspects of language are often treated in similar ways they will be dealt with together here.

It is suggested that the students' attention be drawn very carefully to the way language is used in the text to perform certain functions. They thus see that they are not merely studying grammar but are studying a language whose use is exemplified in the text.

When studying the charts, before doing the exercises that follow them, it is suggested that the teacher might point out the grammatically tricky aspects of the language. An example of this is on page 43 where the chart includes *X has no alternative but to DO* . . . A common mistake with this construction is the omission of *but*. This can be pointed out to the student as he studies the chart, helping him to avoid the mistake in the future.

The exercises that follow, for example, ADVICE, are designed for classroom use. It is suggested that the controlled exercises that usually begin the exploitation should be done orally; indeed, most of the exercises are suitable for oral use, but to provide variety it is often a good idea to make the students write one or two sentences from a particular exploitation. Where, at the end of each section, the practice is of a freer nature, group-work is often very profitable.

As was said in the GENERAL INTRODUCTION, constraints of time may make it impossible to do all the work in class. For this reason there is a key at the back of the book, and parts of the units can be set as homework/self-study.

Where material from the RESOURCES FILE is appropriate to the language being studied a note will be found in the unit, and the material can then be used as a more interesting, or extra, or alternative, stimulus for the students.

TOPIC VOCABULARY

In this section the student is presented with a vocabulary area. This section is not intended for classroom use; the student should discover the meaning of the words him/herself. Teaching vocabulary is usually a fruitless exercise, and would certainly be so here. The exercises which follow the section, however, could be set as homework. It is suggested that all the students be equipped with a good dictionary.

WRITING TASKS

The main objective of these tasks is that the student should practise what he has learnt. Students must be encouraged therefore to use the language from the units. One way of doing this is to put a tick on the page every time the student uses language he has studied from this book. The Option Boxes simply provide more composition titles, should they be needed.

THE RESOURCES FILE

As has been already pointed out, the RESOURCES FILE can be used as a source of extra practice material, particularly where this is suggested. Its main function, however, is to provide interesting and real material for revision. Suggestions will be found under each item, but teachers should feel free to exploit this material as they see fit.

MARKETING CONSULTANCY SERVICES	North Africa Division Hamra Street Beirut, Lebanon
Tel: 725380	Telex: 52413

Mr J.K. Farringdon,
Sales Director,
World Motor-cycles Ltd.,
Dudley Drive,
Birmingham,   22nd August.
United Kingdom.

Dear Mr Farringdon,

We are writing in reply to your letter of August 2nd, which was
passed on to us by MCS Head Office in London. In your letter, you
asked for our advice concerning the marketing of motor-cycles in
North African countries, in particular Tunisia.

5 At the moment, it would seem to us that it is not possible to give
a definitive answer about the prospects for such a plan. This is
especially so, since, in our opinion, there are such vast differences
between the various countries in this area. It would appear to us
that your best course would be to have an area sales survey made, a
10 task we would gladly undertake on your behalf. At the same time as
finding out about sales prospects, it is essential that possible future
dealers should also be investigated, and this service is part of all
sales-surveys we make.

In addition to having a survey made, we would also advise you to make
15 a personal visit to the area, perhaps while the survey team is making
its investigations. This would enable you to 'get the feel' of the
countries concerned, which, in our opinion, is vital for any
businessman planning a major marketing venture.

We look forward to hearing from you again in the near future. If you
20 need any details about the kind of survey we undertake, Head Office
will be very happy to supply them.

Yours sincerely,

C. Clark

1

ADVICE AND OPINION

A | Exercises on the text

1 VOCABULARY ⓚ

Find words or phrases in the text that mean:
a) advertising and selling a commodity
b) an organisation giving professional advice
c) sure and final
d) chances of success
e) very great
f) investigation to find out the chances of selling something
g) for you
h) people who sell for an organisation
i) extremely important

2 TALKING POINTS ⓚ

Say whether the following statements are true or false. If you think the answer is false, give your reasons.
a) Mr Farringdon's letter arrived at the Head Office on August 2nd.
b) Mr Farringdon's letter asked for advice about selling motor-bikes in North African market-squares.
c) Marketing Consultancy Services cannot yet say whether it is a good idea to sell motor-cycles in North African countries.
d) Mr Farringdon won't be able to sell motor-cycles in all North African countries because they are so different from each other.
e) Mr Farringdon is advised to make an area sales-survey.
f) When MCS do sales-surveys, they also find out about places which could sell the articles concerned.
g) MCS think that it is important for businessmen to visit areas where they want to sell things.
h) If Mr Farringdon writes to Head Office asking for details, he will make them very happy.

3 WRITING POINTS ⓚ

Answer the following questions with complete sentences.
a) Why did Mr Farringdon write to MCS?
b) What reasons do MCS give for being unable to answer Mr Farringdon's questions about marketing?
c) What advice do MCS give about finding out whether marketing prospects are good?
d) What do MCS advise Mr Farringdon to do personally, and why?

4 CONTEXT QUESTIONS ⓚ

a) 'Such a plan' in line 6 refers to ...
b) 'This area' in line 8 refers to ...
c) What does 'this service' in line 12 refer to?

2

d) What does 'which' in line 17 refer to?

e) 'Them' in line 21 refers to . . .

5 SUMMARY WORK

Imagine you are Mr Farringdon. You are preparing a very short memorandum for the other directors of World Motor-cycles Ltd. on the advice given by MCS. Write the report in not more than 50 words.

B | Advice

1 Look at the following ways of giving advice, some of which appear in the text.

> I would $\begin{Bmatrix} \text{advise} \\ \text{recommend} \end{Bmatrix}$ you to *DO* . . .
>
> If you take my advice you will *DO* . . .
> If I were you I would *DO* . . . ⟨*informal*⟩

Susan Fisher is a student who is about to leave school. Use the following to give her advice about her future.

a) advise/learn/foreign languages

b) my advice/continue/study

c) recommend/get/job as soon as possible

d) if I/you/go/night-school/learn/profession

e) advise/earn enough money/travel round the world

f) if/you/work/shop with your father

g) my advice/get married, settle down/have a family

Now make more sentences of your own, using the language in this section, in which you give advice to

a) Someone whose new car keeps going wrong

b) Someone whose pet tiger has vanished

c) Someone whose wife/husband spends most of her/his time away from home

2 Look at more ways of giving advice (some of which appear in the text) in which the writer/speaker gives his opinion before giving his advice.

OPINION	ADVICE
In my opinion As far as I'm concerned From my point of view I think	you should *DO* . . . the best thing you can *DO* . . . is *DO* . . .
It would $\begin{Bmatrix} \text{seem} \\ \text{appear} \end{Bmatrix}$ (to me) that	your best course would be to *DO* . . . ⟨*formal*⟩

ADVICE AND OPINION

a. Now you are giving opinions and advice to someone whose neighbours are always holding parties and throwing litter over the fence. ⓚ
   a) seem/me/best course/tell them how/feel
   b) point/view/should call/police
   c) opinion/throw/rubbish back
   d) seem/best course/letter/complaint
   e) as far/concerned/best thing/take them/court
   f) appear/best course/lawyer
   g) opinion/sue them/damages/nervous disorder due to the continual noise

b. Now make more sentences of your own, using language from this section, in which you give advice to
   a) Someone who dresses shabbily, has untidy hair, seldom washes, and gets turned down at all the interviews he/she goes for
   b) Someone who has been accused, by one of his/her colleagues, of embezzling money, even though it is not true
   c) Someone who is having problems with his/her English

3 Look at the following ways of asking for advice.

What* do you $\left\{ \begin{array}{l} \text{advise} \\ \text{recommend} \end{array} \right\}$ me to *DO?*

Could you give me some advice about *DOING?*

Where* $\left\{ \begin{array}{l} \text{can} \\ \text{should} \end{array} \right\}$ I *DO?* ⟨*slightly informal*⟩

* Other WH–questions are also common, e.g. *How/when,* etc.

a. Using the language from the chart above ask for advice in the following situations
   a) You want to know where to live in England in a rural area, but near London
   b) You want advice about learning a musical instrument – i.e. you do not want to learn a very difficult one
   c) You have been offered two jobs. One is in a nice town but the pay is low, the other is well-paid, but in a horrible area
   d) When you try to be nice to your children, they are rude to you
   e) You want to give up smoking, but you do not know how to

4 Below are five situations in which people need advice. Using the language from **1, 2** and **3** (on pages 3 and 4), imagine you are writing the letters in which advice is asked for and given.

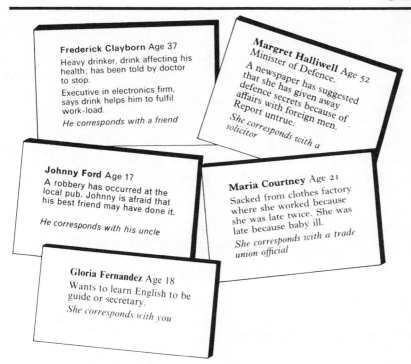

Frederick Clayborn Age 37
Heavy drinker, drink affecting his
health; has been told by doctor
to stop.
Executive in electronics firm,
says drink helps him to fulfil
work-load.
He corresponds with a friend

Margret Halliwell Age 52
Minister of Defence.
A newspaper has suggested
that she has given away
defence secrets because of
affairs with foreign men.
Report untrue.
*She corresponds with a
solicitor*

Johnny Ford Age 17
A robbery has occurred at the
local pub. Johnny is afraid that
his best friend may have done it.
He corresponds with his uncle

Maria Courtney Age 21
Sacked from clothes factory
where she worked because
she was late twice. She was
late because baby ill.
*She corresponds with a trade
union official*

Gloria Fernandez Age 18
Wants to learn English to be
guide or secretary.
She corresponds with you

Resources file references 1 C2 caption b)   2 G2 caption a)

c | Sentence construction

FUTURE TIME CLAUSES
Look at the following sentence from the text

'. . . we would also advise you to make a personal visit to the area, perhaps
while the survey team is making its investigations.' (Lines 14–16)

The second part of the sentence refers to the future, but the present
continuous tense is used because it is a TIME CLAUSE beginning with *while*.
The sentence is produced in the following way:

We would also advise you to make   Perhaps the survey team *will be*
a personal visit to the area.   *making* its investigations *(then)*.

Depending on the situation and context, there are four possible tense forms
which can appear in TIME CLAUSES

> you *DO (Present Simple)*
> you *ARE DOING (Present Continuous)*
> you *HAVE DONE (Present Perfect Simple)*
> you *HAVE BEEN DOING (Present Perfect Continuous)*

ADVICE AND OPINION

EXAMPLES

i) You will meet Tom / He will arrive } **WHEN** — You will meet Tom *when he arrives.*

ii) I can mention it / I will be talking to Jack } **WHILE** — I can mention it *while I am talking to Jack.*

iii) Don't come / I will have had my lunch } **UNTIL** — Don't come *until I have had my lunch.*

iv) You will get to know our methods / You will have been working here for a while } **WHEN** — You will get to know our methods *when you have been working here for a while.*

1 Imagine you have been made redundant, and you are being given (K) information at an unemployment office. Combine the following pairs of sentences in the same way as in the examples.
   a) You will get welfare money.
      You will get a new job. — TILL/UNTIL
   b) You will be able to find work.
      The economic situation will have improved. — AS SOON AS/ONCE
   c) Would you fill in this form?
      You will be waiting. — WHILE
   d) You can apply for help with your rent payments. — AS SOON AS
      You will have been receiving welfare money for a month.
   e) We will also help you. — WHEN
      Your children will need to buy school books.
   f) Please inform us. — IMMEDIATELY
      You will be offered a new job.

2 In the following sentences people are talking about their forthcoming holidays. Complete the sentences with a suitable time clause.
   a) When ____, you'll need a long holiday.
   b) I'll be lying in the sun, while ____.
   c) As soon as ____, my own holidays will be starting.
   d) I'm going to book my flight immediately ____.
   e) Is there any chance of you seeing my father, while ____?
   f) By the time ____, you'll be too tired to enjoy your holidays.
   g) I'm not going to work so hard, once ____.
   h) You'd better learn to drive properly, before ____ or you'll get arrested.

6

3 Here is an advertisement for a career in banking. Imagine you are giving information about job prospects to someone who is thinking of taking up the career.

:nager

ationally oriented
ι in Kuwait. The
ving within a fast
:ondary objective
parate subsidiary
·lent full service

A CAREER IN BANKING?

Salary £2,400 rising to £4,800 after 7 years. In-service training. Special 1 month course in London after 1 year's service. Low interest loans for house-purchasers with no minimum service requirement. Satisfactory experience in all departments leads to automatic consideration for deputy manager's post. Free medical insurance after 3 months' service. *Please reply in complete confidence to Mr Hurst, Recruitment Officer.*

e.g. *When you start, you will be earning at least £2,400 a year.*

Resources file reference B1 caption a)

D | Structure and style

There are a number of adjectives which, when used in the pattern
It is ADJECTIVE that...
often use SHOULD with the verb in the 'that-clause'.
In the text, line 12, there is the clause
'... *it is essential* that possible dealers *should* also be investigated ...'
This pattern occurs after adjectives expressing
Surprise and shock (e.g. *amazing, horrifying, crazy,* etc.)
Disapproval and disappointment (e.g. *typical, sad,* etc.)
Advisability and importance (e.g. *better, essential, vital,* etc.)
Justice (e.g. *(only) fair, (only) natural,* etc.)
The main use of this pattern is to comment on an idea rather than on a fact, and such sentences with 'should' are rather subjective.

EXAMPLE Compare
i) It is surprising that you believe him.
   = *The* FACT *that you believe him is surprising.*
ii) It is surprising that you should believe him.
   = JUST THE IDEA *of you believing him is surprising.*
(Although in many cases there is very little, if any difference, between a

ADVICE AND OPINION

sentence with 'should' and one without, an advanced student ought to begin to note examples where 'should' is used and try to imitate them.)

1 Rewrite the following sentences beginning with 'It is ADJECTIVE that . . .' Ⓚ

    EXAMPLE   You know my uncle. That is rather odd.
          It is rather odd that you should know my uncle.

a) Children are allowed so much freedom. That is crazy.
b) It is essential for children to be taught discipline.
c) It is only natural for parents to spoil their children.
d) It is extremely important for children to learn to share things.
e) No two children learn in the same way. This is strange.
f) It is much better for parents to know about the problems their children have at school.
g) It is only right for parents to get involved in the education of their children.
h) Some parents consider school a waste of time. This is sad.

2 Many people are worried about the increase in noise and air pollution in towns. Imagine you believe that noise and air pollution should be reduced. Make statements on the subject beginning as follows
a) It is only fair that . . .
b) It is typical that . . .
c) It is horrifying that . . .
d) It is absurd that . . .
e) It is unfortunate that . . .
f) It is absolutely vital that . . .
g) It is only reasonable that . . .
h) It is quite incredible that . . .

E | Topic vocabulary

1 CONSUMER VOCABULARY
Using a dictionary or any other source find out the meaning of the following words connected with advertising, buying and selling.
a) market; to market
b) product; article
c) advertise; advert(isement); commercial; advertising campaign
d) to hire; to rent; hire-purchase (agreement)
e) guarantee
f) reduction; to reduce; cut-price; value (for money)
g) second-hand; shop-soiled; bargain; to be (not) worth it
h) badly-made; well-made; to last; to break down; to wear out

2 Using the vocabulary from **1** above, complete the blanks in the following sentences

Ⓚ

a) 'Woof' dog food has started a new advertising ____. They have put ____ in the newspapers and ____ on the television.

b) Somebody owned my car before me, so it is ____.

c) 'Smooth' shirts are ____. You can still wear them after ten years because they never ____.

d) If you are going to buy a new camera, make sure you get a ____ so that you can have it repaired free for the first year.

e) The department store is holding a sale. Prices have been ____, so that everything is very cheap. You can pick up some really fantastic ____.

f) They are not ____ buying. They are ____ and they only ____ for two months.

3 Now write sentences of your own (using consumer vocabulary) about things you have bought recently.

F | Writing tasks

150–200 words

1 You want to make a career as a tourist guide, and since you speak English you would obviously be interested in working with English-speaking tourists. Write a letter to the British Embassy in your country asking for advice about the best way to achieve this ambition.

2 OPTION BOX

a) A letter to an English person who is coming to stay in your country for two months. Give them advice about clothes, money, etc.

b) A letter to someone you know in England asking for advice about where to study English. You should explain why you want to continue with English, and what sort of things you want to do, etc.

Resources file reference E2 caption c)

34, Clareville Mansions,
Trebelwyn,
Nr. Wadebridge,
Cornwall.

9th November.

Dear Mr Huntley,

I am writing to you in your capacity as the Member of Parliament
for this constituency about a matter which has angered and worried
many of us who live in Trebelwyn and nearby.

5 We have always known about the Craven Hill government research
station, two miles from this village, and until a month ago we
had always believed that it was used for the purpose of
agricultural investigation. But as you must be aware, the recent
revelations in the Sunday Star, and the comments which the Prime
10 Minister made mean we now know for certain that Craven Hill is
used for the development of materials for biological warfare.

A lot of us have become extremely alarmed by this, and we have
formed a group called 'Craven Hill Action Group'. I am the
appointed leader and I am therefore writing to you to ask for
15 help. Many of the members of our group have very strong moral
objections to the idea of biological warfare. It is frightening
to realise that a small test-tube full of germs could destroy a
whole civilisation. Even those, however, who do not feel strongly
about this are determined to get the Craven Hill station closed
20 down so that our families and children do not have to live in
fear of some terrible accident.

We are asking, therefore, for your help. In two weeks' time we
are holding an afternoon fete to raise money for our campaign,
and in the evening some of our members will be putting on a
25 concert. We were wondering if it would be possible for you to
come and meet us, and maybe give a speech since we know that you
have spoken against nuclear and biological warfare, and you are a
man whose outspoken views on this subject are well known. If you
are not able to join us then we would like to come to London and
30 visit you at the House of Commons, and we were wondering what day
would be most convenient for you.

We are looking forward to hearing from you.

Yours sincerely,

Kenneth Pringle

Kenneth Pringle
Craven Hill Action Group

PLANS AND ARRANGEMENTS

A | Exercises on the text

1 VOCABULARY Ⓚ
Find words or phrases in the text that mean:
a) position
b) an area that elects one member of Parliament
c) concerned with the land and farming
d) disclosures, surprising new facts
e) organise, put together
f) feelings that something is bad, against somebody's principles
g) an open-air sale run by people who are not shopkeepers, which tries to raise money

2 TALKING POINTS Ⓚ
Say whether the following statements about the text are true or false. If you think the answer is false, give your reasons.
a) Mr Huntley is a politician.
b) Craven Hill investigates agriculture.
c) All the villagers are members of the Action Group.
d) Some members of the group think it is wrong to use biological weapons.
e) The group thinks that Craven Hill endangers local people.
f) The group wants Mr Huntley to play in their concert.
g) The group wishes to arrange a meeting in London with Mr Huntley.

3 WRITING POINTS Ⓚ
Answer the following questions with complete sentences.
a) What is Mr Huntley, and who does he represent?
b) What is 'biological warfare'?
c) How could a 'small test-tube full of germs' destroy a whole civilisation?

4 CONTEXT QUESTIONS Ⓚ
a) Who is 'us' in line 3?
b) What does 'it' refer to in line 6?
c) Who are 'those' in line 17?
d) Whose families are 'our families' in line 19?

5 SUMMARY WORK
Imagine you are one of the 'Craven Hill Action Group'. You want to place an advertisement in a national newspaper explaining what you are and what you object to. You hope that the advertisement will bring a lot of people to your next meeting. Advertisements are expensive, so you must limit your words to 60. Write the advertisement, using ONLY information from the text.

11

PLANS AND ARRANGEMENTS

B | Revision-test

1 Join the following pairs of sentences to make one sentence.
   a) John will not stop working.
   He will have finished what he is doing.
   b) He will stop work.
   He will go and have a drink.
   c) He will feel a little drunk.
   He will have been drinking for a couple of hours.   (3 marks)

2 Change each of the following sentences so that they start with the phrases given.
   a) 'Give up drinking'   If I were you . . .
   b) 'Stop smoking so many cigarettes'   It would appear . . .
   c) 'How can I stop smoking?'   Can you give me . . .
   d) 'Eat sweets instead'   In my opinion . . .   (4 marks)

3 Choose the right answer, A, B, C, or D in the following questions.
   a) When he got a job, he had no difficulty in ____ his family.
   A buying   B deserting   c supporting   D holding up
   b) When the factory closed down he was ____.
   A sacked   B made redundant   c fired   D given unemployment
   c) This was very serious because he had signed a ____ agreement for a new car.
   A rent   B hire-purchase   c second-hand   D shop-soiled   (3 marks)

4 Write three sentences to someone whose son has run away from home, and has disappeared. You should use
                          Advice language   (5 marks)
                          Time clauses   (Total: 15 marks)

C | Arrangements and invitations

1 MAKING ARRANGEMENTS
Look at the following ways of making arrangements some of which occur in the text.

I was wondering $\begin{Bmatrix} \text{if} \\ \text{whether} \end{Bmatrix}$ I wonder	Monday would be $\begin{Bmatrix} \text{convenient} \\ \text{possible} \end{Bmatrix}$ for you we could *DO* . . . on Monday. it would be possible for *X* to *DO* . . .
Would it be $\begin{Bmatrix} \text{possible} \\ \text{convenient} \end{Bmatrix}$ for *X* to *DO* . . . on Monday? Could *X DO* . . . on Monday? ⟨*slightly informal*⟩	

12

PLANS AND ARRANGEMENTS

Use the following to make arrangements.

a) I wonder/we/meet/Friday
b) Would/possible/me/see you/Tuesday
c) Could you come/my house next week
d) I/wondering/possible/you/visit us/the summer
e) we/lunch together next week
f) Would/convenient/me/pay you/visit/Thursday
g) I wonder/Friday/convenient/you
h) we have/drink together/Saturday

2 EXTENDING INVITATIONS

> Would you like to *DO* . . .?
> Would you be interested in *DOING* . . .?

Use the following to extend invitations.

a) you like/stay with us next weekend
b) you/interested/going/theatre next Thursday
c) come to a party/Friday
d) going hitch-hiking/summer

3 RESPONDING TO ARRANGEMENTS AND INVITATIONS

No	
I am afraid	I will not be able to *DO* . . . I can not manage to *DO* . . . it will not be possible for *X* to *D* . . . TIME will not be convenient
Yes	I would be delighted to *DO* . . . It will be possible for *X* to *DO* . . . ⟨*weak*⟩ I would love to *DO* . . . ⟨*slightly informal*⟩

Below are some situations concerning invitations or arrangements. Say what you would write in each case.

a) A friend has asked you to stay for the weekend. You wish to accept.
b) The gas board have written you a letter asking if they can come and 'read your meter' on Thursday. This would be a bad day for you.
c) You have written to an English company for a job interview. They replied, asking you to go at 12.30 next Wednesday. You wish to confirm the appointment.
d) A friend has asked you if you could arrange a party for some visitors he has. You cannot.
e) You have been asked to a concert by one of your distant relations. You accept.

PLANS AND ARRANGEMENTS

4 George is a student who is in his last term at college. He is trying to get a job teaching. Below is his diary for the next two weeks.

July

4 Monday Week 37
12.00 Lunch with Peter

5 Tuesday
Interview at school for teaching job 15.30

6 Wednesday
11.00 Literature lecture
14.00 Politics seminar

7 Thursday PAYE Week 23
Evening Pub with Jenny and Mark

8 Friday
16.00 Tutorial with Professor Bradbury

9 Saturday *Afternoon Football match with Chris*

10 Sunday 15th after Trinity

July

11 Monday Week 38
Evening Cinema with Jenny

12 Tuesday

13 Wednesday
11.00 Literature lecture
14.00 Politics seminar

14 Thursday PAYE Week 24
Interview at a school for teaching job. 11.30

15 Friday
16.00 Tutorial with Professor Bradbury

16 Saturday

17 Sunday 16th after Trinity
Lunch with Jenny's parents

Using the language of ARRANGEMENTS and INVITATIONS write sentences from the letters between George and others. George will refuse an invitation if he has something arranged for that time.

a) George's bank manager wants to see him at 11.00 on Wednesday the 6th.
b) A school wants George to go for an interview during the afternoon of Thursday the 7th.
c) Jenny's parents invite George for lunch on Sunday the 10th.
d) George's landlord wants to call and see him on the morning of Tuesday the 12th.
e) George's maiden aunt wants to have dinner with him on the evening of Monday the 11th.
f) Professor Bradbury wants to change the time of the tutorial to 12.00 on Thursday the 14th.
g) One of George's lecturers invites George to go sailing on Saturday the 16th.
h) George's bank manager now wants to see him on the morning of Friday the 15th.

Resources file references   1 D1 caption b)   2 D2 caption a)

14

D | Sentence construction

RELATIVE CLAUSES – DEFINING

In using relative (*who, that, which*, etc.) clauses you need to concentrate on the following points:

i) when it is necessary to have a relative pronoun, and when it can be left out;

ii) whether the style is ⟨*informal*⟩ or ⟨*formal*⟩

Look at the following examples from the text and notice when the relative is the subject, when it is the object of the following verb, and when it is a possessive.

SUBJECT   ... *a matter which has angered and worried many of us* (l. 2)

OBJECT   ... *the comments which the Prime Minister made* ... (l. 8/9)

POSSESSIVE ... *a man whose outspoken views on this subject* ... (l. 27)

The basic rules for using relatives can be summarised as follows.

People and pets

	Subject	*Object*	*Possessive*	*With preposition*
⟨INFORMAL⟩	that (who)	* (that)	whose	* (that) ... PREPOSITION
⟨FORMAL⟩	who	who(m)	whose	who ... PREPOSITION PREPOSITION whom ⟨*very formal*⟩

Things

⟨INFORMAL⟩	that	* (that)	whose	* (that) ... PREPOSITION
⟨FORMAL⟩	which	which	(of which) ⟨*very formal*⟩	preposition+which

* Cases where no relative is used are known as contact clauses. (The words in brackets are the less usual forms.)

In many cases the idea of possession is shown by a *with*-phrase,

e.g. $A \left\{ \begin{matrix} man \\ car \end{matrix} \right\}$ *with big* $\left\{ \begin{matrix} ears. \\ headlights. \end{matrix} \right\}$

     is more common than

     $A \left\{ \begin{matrix} man \\ car \end{matrix} \right\}$ *whose* $\left\{ \begin{matrix} ears \\ headlights \end{matrix} \right\}$ *are big.*

1   Make the following pairs or groups of sentences into one sentence by using relative or contact clauses and omitting the word in italics. Write each sentence in the style indicated.   Ⓚ

PLANS AND ARRANGEMENTS

EXAMPLE

One member of Parliament was very helpful. I spoke to him. ⟨formal⟩
I spoke to one member of Parliament *who* was very helpful.

a) The other day I bumped into an old friend of mine. *He* now works in the car trade. ⟨informal⟩

b) My friend suggested going for a drink in a pub. He knew *one*. ⟨informal⟩

c) The pub was a kind of cellar. *Its* tables were old and wooden. ⟨informal⟩

d) I was amazed at some of the stories. He told *them* about the car trade. ⟨informal⟩

e) It would seem that there are a few real criminals in the trade. The police know all about *them*. But *they* are very difficult to catch. ⟨formal⟩

f) Most of the criminals work in gangs. *Their* leaders tend to prefer driving sports cars. ⟨formal⟩

g) Many of the car dealers make their money by respraying stolen cars before selling them. Jack was talking about *these car dealers*. ⟨formal⟩

2 Add a relative clause to the word in italics to define it more exactly. Make your sentences either ⟨formal⟩ or ⟨informal⟩.

EXAMPLE I particularly dislike *people* . . .

⟨formal⟩   i) *I particularly dislike people who encourage their children to misbehave.*

⟨informal⟩ ii) *I particularly dislike people that let their children shout and scream.*

a) Recently I met *someone* _____ .

b) Where is that *book* _____ .

c) *Food* _____ is very expensive.

d) Students prefer *teachers* _____ .

e) *Cars* _____ are very annoying.

f) *Grandparents* _____ are often unhappy.

g) I asked for the *suit* _____ .

h) That woman is the *one* _____ .

i) I can still remember the *visit* _____ .

E | Structure and style

IT IS *ADJECTIVE+INFINITIVE*

Look at the following sentence from the text.

It is frightening to realise that a small test-tube full of germs could destroy a whole civilisation. (Lines 15–17)

16

PLANS AND ARRANGEMENTS

This is a combination of the following two sentences

  i) A small test-tube full of terms could destroy a whole civilisation.
 ii) When anyone realises this, it is frightening/Realising this is frightening.

1 Join the following pairs of sentences in the same way. Ⓚ
  a) Someone from our country has won a gold medal. It is exciting when anyone hears this.
  b) Some parents maltreat their children. Believing this is hard.
  c) A spider spins its web. When we see how this is done, it is fascinating.
  d) More and more young people are going to university. When anyone sees this, it is encouraging.
  e) One day people will be living on Venus. Visualising this is difficult.

2 Make sentences in the same way about the following situations (your sentences should reflect your personal opinions).
  a) More and more couples are getting divorced
  b) Medical research is being expanded
  c) You have passed an important examination
  d) Our ancestors were apes
  e) We sometimes think we have experienced something before, when in fact we have not
  f) Americans were English once

F | Topic vocabulary

ENTERTAINMENT

1 Below are words connected with different types of entertainment. Find out what they mean, using a dictionary or any other source.

a. *Places and types*
  a) theatre; cinema; night-club; hall
  b) concert; play; show; cabaret; festival; circus; fair

b. *Theatre*
  a) comedy; tragedy; farce
  b) stage; wings; auditorium; orchestra pit; scenery
  c) curtain; act; scene; interval

c. *Music*
  a) pop; classical; choral; jazz; folk; opera
  b) theme; movement; symphony; concerto
  c) improvise; improvisation; live (adj.); solo

d. *General*
  a) put on; perform; take part in
  b) (go on) tour; booking; date; run

PLANS AND ARRANGEMENTS

2 Use appropriate words from the list above to complete the blanks in the following sentences. (K)

a) The first time Paul saw Maria, she was _____ in a play. She had the main female role.

b) The play was a _____. It was very funny, and Paul, who was sitting in the _____ watching, couldn't help laughing.

c) The next night Paul went to a _____ concert, with the famous saxophonist Bill Blowitt. Paul had never seen him _____ before, he had only heard him on records.

d) Later that week Paul went back to watch Maria. She first appeared from the _____ at the side of the stage for her scene in the first _____. She got married at the end of the play, just before the _____ fell.

e) After the _____ Paul met Maria, and asked her if she wanted to go dancing in a _____, where there was a _____ with a famous comedian.

G | Writing tasks

150–200 words

1 You are a newspaper reporter, and you want to interview an English politician who is visiting your country. Write a letter asking for an appointment with him next week (you should state when you are available and when you are not).

2 OPTION BOX

a) A letter to an English friend, inviting him/her to stay with you.
b) A letter to your bank manager, asking for an appointment next week.
c) You have been invited to stay with an American friend who lives in your country. You would like to take your sister with you because she has nothing to do at present and would otherwise be left alone in the house. Write accepting the invitation, asking if you can take your sister.

Resources file references   1 A2 caption c)   2 G2 caption b)

oman
or her
hird at
ird is
enings
'uring
ee to
way
rand-
enter-
d, but
rmous
ie vast
lation,
ontent
gling
y go
n be
ias a.
fact,
that
mous
arity,
ihood
ing in
: have
e must

tele-
ying
—a
lass
best
de-
iany
hear
rks,
last
hich
had
etri-
ɔnal
ave
ɔre
fect
ides.
ular
g a
our

ibly
ied
i in
yes.
ɔtly

FOLLOWING his release last week after more than a fortnight in the hands of kidnappers, the managing director of the massive Portmann Industrial Electrics combine, Mr George Myers has told the story of his terrifying ordeal to the SUNDAY STAR. Here then is the EXCLUSIVE story, as told by Mr Myers.

Death wagon ordeal

LOOKING back over those terrible weeks—most of the time flat on my back with my hands tied—I would say that the most difficult thing to bear was the inactivity. I could only think of death, which was staring me in the face. I made myself think of the happy
5 times I had had, but I kept thinking of my life as grains of sand in an hour-glass; I had no idea how much time I had left.

The kidnap had clearly been planned meticulously. As I was taking my usual evening stroll with the dog, a rather well-
10 dressed man came up to me and asked me to direct him to the local church hall. I was just turning round to point up the road when a wet cloth was pressed over my nose . . . that was the last I knew until I
15 came to in the back of a large van of some kind. It was only after I realised we were moving that I remembered what had happened. Still groggy from the chloroform I tried to sit up, but I was firmly
20 strapped to a narrow bed.

As soon as we stopped, the back door was thrown open and in jumped two men. The light of their torches blinded me, but as I got used to it I recognised the man
25 who had stopped me in the street. I felt that he was sneering at me, and as the days went by, I discovered that James—as he was known—was the most heartless, calculating person I had ever had the
30 misfortune to meet. I immediately asked what they meant to do with me, to which he replied that it all depended on whether my company would pay the ransom money. I asked to be allowed to get in

Turn to Page 6 Column 5

19

PERMISSION

From Page 2

35 touch with my wife, as I knew she would be terribly worried, and it was then that I found out just how nasty James was. 'Feel free', he said, and got out of the van, 40 chuckling to himself at his little joke.

I suddenly had what I thought was a brilliant idea. For several years I have been taking pills for my heart, so I decided to feign an attack. Breathing heavily and 45 clutching my throat, I shouted that I was having a heart-attack, and that I needed my pills. You can imagine my surprise when James came in with a glass of water, and a bottle of my special pills. How long 50 had they been keeping tabs on me, I wondered, to know so much about my personal life? Having given me the pills, James told his accomplice to let me have something to eat while he 'arranged things'. 55 As, in the position I was in, I couldn't move, I asked them to untie me, and to let me use my hands. The accomplice undid the straps that kept me tied to the bed, but he wouldn't free my hands.

60 When James returned, he was carrying a small cassette recorder. With thinly-veiled sarcasm he asked me if I would mind reading a short typed message to my firm, explaining my situation, and demanding 65 a substantial ransom for my release. Once again, I begged to be permitted to make a recording to send to my wife, and you can imagine how my heart sank when he told me that the only thing my wife might 70 receive was my wedding ring—with my finger still in it.

By this time I was beginning to feel the 'call of nature', and I asked if I could use the toilet. James agreed readily, lifted 75 down a plastic bucket from the side of the van, and untied my legs. They refused to leave me alone even for a couple of minutes . . . my humiliation and de-moralisation were complete.

The second part of George Myers' dramatic story will be in next week's SUNDAY STAR. Make sure you don't miss it. ORDER YOUR COPY NOW!

A | Exercises on the text

1 VOCABULARY (K)
Find words or phrases in the text that mean:
a) extremely carefully
b) with very unclear thoughts (because of alcohol or drugs)
c) having no feelings
d) unpleasant (of a person)
e) laughing softly
f) pretend
g) someone who helps (usually in a crime)
h) the feeling that you have lost your dignity

2 TALKING POINTS (K)
Say whether the following statements about the text are true or false. If you think the answer is false, give your reasons.
a) The kidnappers wanted to know where the church hall was.
b) James had an unpleasant sense of humour.
c) They would not let Myers send a message to his wife.
d) Myers needed his pills.
e) James wanted to cut off Myers' ring finger.
f) They let Myers have something to eat.
g) They let Myers go out to the lavatory.
h) They ordered Myers to read a prepared statement.

3 WRITING POINTS Ⓚ

Answer the following questions with complete sentences.

a) What did Myers usually do in the evenings?

b) Who stopped Myers and asked him the way to the church hall?

c) Where was the bed that Myers was strapped to?

d) Why was Myers surprised when James brought the pills?

4 CONTEXT QUESTIONS Ⓚ

a) 'He' in line 32 refers to . . .

b) What moment is referred to by 'then' in line 36?

c) What does 'it' refer to in line 32?

d) Who is 'he' in line 53?

e) '. . . those terrible weeks' (line 1). Which terrible weeks?

5 SUMMARY WORK

a) What does Myers ask for permission to do in the story?

b) Change each of the incidents from **5a** – with the kidnappers' answers – back into dialogue form.

B | Revision–test

1 In the following sentences, complete the blanks and put the correct form of the words in the brackets.

a) 'Would it be ＿＿ for you (come) and see me on Thursday evening?'

b) 'I'm afraid I ＿＿ Thursday, but I (love) to come some other day.'

c) '(Come) you on Monday? I'd like you to meet the man ＿＿ was at Jeff's party.'

d) 'That sounds a good idea. Would you (interest) ＿＿ coming with me sometime next week?'

e) 'I (be) delighted. I want to see that play ＿＿ has had such good reviews.' (10 marks)

2 Rearrange the order of the following words to make sentences.

a) think/Mars/on/may/life/to/it's/there/exciting/be/that.

b) isn't/sure/we/on/life/Mars/landed/man/there/can't/be/that/until/there / has. (2 marks)

3 Write sentences:

a) asking someone to meet you next Friday

b) asking someone for advice about where to study

b) giving your opinion about where to study

d) telling someone that you will not be able to meet them on Friday

(8 marks)

(Total: 20 marks)

PERMISSION

c | Permission

1 In the passage you have just read, Myers often asks to be *allowed to* do things; we often use *to be not allowed to* to say what we cannot do.

EXAMPLE *You are not allowed to park on a double yellow line.*

Below are signs in a park. Say what you (impersonal) are not allowed to do there.

2 When we talk about permission we say what we could/could not do, and what we can/cannot do. Below are some ways of saying this.

a) Describes whether we could or not

> allow *X* to *DO* . . .
> (Will not allow *X* to *DO* . . .)
> (Will not let *X DO* . . .)
> to be $\begin{Bmatrix} \text{allowed} \\ \text{permitted} \end{Bmatrix}$ to *DO* . . .

b) Describes the ACT of saying yes or no

> give *X* permission to *DO* . . .
> (Will not give *X* permission to *DO* . . .)
> to be $\begin{Bmatrix} \text{given} \\ \text{refused} \end{Bmatrix}$ permission to *DO* . . .

a. Re-write the following sentences starting with the words given. Use language from *(a)* and *(b)* above.

PERMISSION

EXAMPLE

Yesterday Mary's father said she could stay out late.
Mary's father *gave her permission to stay out late*.
Now do these in the same way.

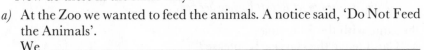

a) At the Zoo we wanted to feed the animals. A notice said, 'Do Not Feed the Animals'.
   We _____

b) Yesterday Anita wanted to go to the cinema with her friend. Her father didn't say no.
   Anita's father _____

c) Yesterday Fred's boss said he could take the day off work to go to his sister's wedding.
   Fred's boss _____

d) Fred's boss told Jake (Fred's friend) that Jake couldn't have the day off to go to his friend's sister's wedding.
   Jake _____

e) Trainers of horses can't give their horses stimulating drugs before races.
   Trainers _____

b. When Jim was in the army, there were a lot of things he could not do, and some he could. Make sentences using the information below about what you think he could/could not do. Start your sentences in one of the ways suggested.

When Jim was in the army . . . One night the sergeant . . . The sergeant . . .	Smoke during lectures. Go out drinking. Take his girlfriend back to the camp. Be absent without permission. Play cards for money in the camp. Go on leave. Tell the sergeant what he thought of him.

Can you think of other things that soldiers can/cannot do in the army?

3 When we ask about permission we report our questions in the following ways

X asked	if *X* could *DO* . . . to be allowed to *DO* . . . for permission to *DO* . . .

and we report the answer to our question in the following ways

He	refused agreed	to	let *X DO* . . . allow *X* to *DO* . . .

and by using expressions from 2 (above)

PERMISSION

Using the language above, change the following into 'reported speech'.

EXAMPLE

> Isabel: 'You can't borrow my pen, Robert.'
> *Isabel refused to let Robert borrow her pen.*

Now do the same with the following.　　　　　　　　　　　　　Ⓚ

a) Gloria: 'Can I leave the class early, please?'
Teacher: 'No.'

b) Fred: 'Can I have my holidays in September?'
Fred's boss: 'Yes, of course you can.'

c) Paula: 'Can I have a permit to stay in the country for three months
longer?'
Immigration official: 'You can't stay in the country any longer unless
you are a full-time student.'

4 Diana Close, of Coastal T.V., took a film crew abroad to make a
documentary. Below is the film schedule she had planned.

Subject: Documentary	Schedule for: D. Close/film-crew
Monday	**A.M.** Military Parade.
	P.M. ~~Soldiers – training.~~
Tuesday	**A.M.** Interview president. ~~President's house~~ ~~and family.~~
	P.M. Secondary school class. Interview principal; ~~schoolchildren.~~
Wednesday	**A.M.** Visit tourist resort. Visit downtown capital ~~(slums?)~~
	P.M. Political rally organised by the government. Interview Minister of Justice ~~Law Courts.~~
Thursday	**A.M.** Interview former president. ~~Visit~~ ~~Mental hospital; prison farm.~~
	P.M. (Evening) Classical music concert. Reactions of audience.

When Close and the film crew reached the country, they found that there
were some things they could do (the government of the country said they
could), and some things they could not. Diana Close crossed out the
things in the schedule that they could not do.

Using the permission language you have studied, imagine that you are
Diana Close telling your boss what you asked to do, and what you could/
could not do.

24

PERMISSION

EXAMPLE

We asked for permission to film the parade on Monday, and we wanted to include pictures of the soldiers training. Well, we were allowed to film the parade, but they refused to let us watch the soldiers training.

Resources file references   1 A2 caption a)   2 A2 caption b)

D | Sentence construction

SUBSTITUTING INFINITIVES FOR RELATIVE CLAUSES

Notice in this sentence from the text, an infinitive is used rather than a relative clause.

The most difficult thing *to bear* (The most difficult thing *which I had to bear*) was the inactivity. (Line 2)

This structure often occurs as a way of avoiding defining relative clauses which *either*

contain the verbs *must, can, could, should, have to*, and *need*

or

define preceding superlatives (*the biggest, the only, the first*, etc.)

EXAMPLES

i)   *Mr Myers has a lot of letters* $\begin{cases} \textit{which he must answer.} \\ \textit{to answer.} \end{cases}$

ii) *The last one* $\begin{cases} \textit{who was caught} \\ \textit{to be caught} \end{cases}$ *was James.*

1 Change the sentences which follow, using an infinitive as illustrated above. Ⓚ

   a) The best way in which you can learn things is by actually doing them yourself.

   b) The first people you should go to when you need help are your friends.

   c) Tenzing and Hillary were the first men who climbed Everest.

   d) Sorry I can't come earlier but I have a lot of arrangements which I have to make.

   e) One of the problems in some urban areas is that children have no parks which they can play in.

   f) Can you imagine anything so frustrating – a bottle of wine and nothing which I could open it with?

   g) There is no way which could prevent the disease from spreading.

2 Manchester is trying to encourage more tourists who visit London to make the journey north. They have printed the following information sheet to be handed out at airports and major stations.

PERMISSION

WELCOME TO MANCHESTER!

Historic places! Friendly people!

LOW PRICE ACCOMMODATION

From London TRAIN $2\frac{1}{2}$ hours £13.00 (ret.)

BUS $4\frac{1}{2}$ hours £5.00 (ret.)

CONNECTIONS TO THE LAKE DISTRICT

**Cathedral   Northern Art Gallery   over 20 cinemas
Library   Theatre   Hallé Orchestra
Restaurants to suit all tastes and pockets**

Further information

The Manchester Bureau

King's Square, London SW1 (near Victoria Station)

Accommodation arranged if desired

Use the above information to make sentences like the following example
If you want to meet friendly people, the place to stay is Manchester.

E | Structure and style

PRESENT AND PERFECT PARTICIPLES—WRITTEN STYLE
Look at the following two sentences from the text

- *a* i) *Breathing* heavily and *clutching* my throat, *I* shouted that I was having a heart-attack. (ll. 43–45)
- *b* i) *Having given* me the pills, *James* told his accomplice to let me have something to eat. (ll. 51–53)

In speech, we would probably express the same ideas as follows

- *a* ii) I started to breathe heavily, clutched my throat, and shouted . . .
- *b* ii) When he'd given me the pills, James told his accomplice . . .

Breathing and *clutching* are both known as PRESENT PARTICIPLES.
Having given is what is known as a PERFECT PARTICIPLE.

Perfect participles are rare in normal spoken English, as are present participles, except when they replace relative clauses. For example, James probably said to Myers (sarcastically)

'Would you mind reading this typed message to your firm
$\begin{cases} \text{which explains} \\ \text{explaining} \end{cases}$ the situation you're in?'

26

Note 1 We only use the PERFECT PARTICIPLE if it is necessary to *show clearly that one action finished before the other one started*. If the writer had used a present participle in (*bi*), how would the meaning have changed?

Note 2 The subject of the participle must be the same as the subject of the main clause. For example, this sentence would be impossible: *Walking through the park, the flowers were beautiful*, since it would mean that the flowers were walking through the park!

1 When George Myers was released, he gave a press conference. He was questioned particularly about his feelings both during his captivity and since his release. Using a present or perfect participle, combine the following pairs of sentences to show how the newspaper reported the interview.

EXAMPLE

'I thought they would kill me if I tried to escape, so I never tried.'

i) *Thinking* they would kill him if he tried to escape, he had never tried.
'I never heard the accomplice's name, so I don't know who he was.'

ii) *Never having heard* the accomplice's name, he didn't know who he was.

a) 'I realised very early on that they were such heartless people, so I did nothing to antagonise them.'

b) 'I tried to reason with James once or twice, but I gave up because it clearly had no effect whatsoever.'

c) 'I sometimes looked at James and realised what greed for money could do to people.'

d) 'I was very close to death at times, and I now know how much I value life.'

e) 'I spent 14 days in captivity and now I am looking forward to a long rest.'

2 Last night you went to a circus. Using present and perfect participles, write sentences about the following things

a) The clowns
b) The lion-tamer
c) The trapeze artist
d) An elephant that got out of control
e) The tight-rope walker

F | Topic vocabulary

CHARACTER

1 Here are some more common adjectives about people's personalities. Find out what each one means, using a dictionary or any other source.

a) good-natured; bad-tempered
b) good-humoured; cheerful

PERMISSION

c) easy-going
d) severe; strict
e) sympathetic; unsympathetic
f) unselfish; selfish (self-centred)
g) considerate; inconsiderate

h) generous; mean
i) well-mannered; ill-mannered
j) self-confident
k) modest; conceited
l) hard-hearted

2 A woman is gossiping to her next-door neighbour about an elderly   Ⓚ
married couple she knows, and about their personalities. Using only
words from the list above, complete the blanks, according to the
explanations she gives either before or afterwards.

'Well, yesterday, I met old Mrs Jones. Lovely old lady she is – always
cheerful and helpful – ever so _(a)_ which is more than I can say about
that husband of hers. He's so _(b)_, arguing and shouting and
complaining all the time. And I thought my husband was _(c)_ until I saw
the way *he* holds on to his money! Not that *she* worries or complains. I've
never known anyone so _(d)_. But he's really _(e)_, I mean he never thinks
about her or what she wants. He's got no feelings at all, the _(f)_ old devil!
They're just so different – if you tell her about your problems, she listens
and tries to understand and gives you advice, you know, very _(g)_. And
it's only because of her that their children have turned out so polite and
charming – such _(h)_ young people! *He* just gave them discipline, told
them what they couldn't do, like some _(i)_ schoolmaster. Still, Mrs Jones
keeps smiling and happy – I don't think I'd be that _(j)_, married to *him*!'

3 Take ten other words from the original list of vocabulary and try to think
of people who you know that you could apply them to. Then write ten
sentences about them, showing from the context why you can use that
word to describe them.

G | Writing tasks
150–200 words

1 Write a composition about a teacher who once taught you. You should
try to include some of the character vocabulary you have been studying,
and some permission language. Start your composition with the words:
'One teacher who I will never forget was . . .'

2 OPTION BOX

> a) An unfortunate experience at the customs.
> b) A journey that took longer than expected.
> c) My grandmother.

Resources file references 1 A1 caption a) 2 D1 caption a)

28

JULIA ELLIOTT discusses the English love of pets and makes some suggestions.

A nation of pet-lovers

A RECENT survey in the United States showed that the average family spent more money on its pets than on its children.
5 Although this is a rather shocking statistic, it should not surprise anyone who has seen the doggy beauty parlours or the quiet shady groves where loved pets of
10 all varieties are laid to rest for ever. It· is possible that the Americans are unique in treating their little friends in this way, but what information we do have
15 would suggest that the English, too, are slavish in their attentions to the whims of their pets.

This can clearly be seen when we look at pet foods, which
20 often contain more vitamins than human food or, at least, are seldom less nutritious. They certainly cost as much. Last year the British public spent two
25 hundred million pounds on pet food alone, to say nothing of veterinary bills and animal furniture. It is difficult not to feel resentful about this when
30 one considers what the same amount could do for victims of starvation and poverty, and so it is not unusual for me to get hot under the collar when I read
35 about another old person who

has left all his/her money to a dog or cat home.

There are a variety of reasons why I, personally, find the
40 popularity of British pets alarming. Among other things they cause physical problems. An example of this is New York where they have great difficulty
45 getting rid of the mess that dogs leave on the streets. Many people find this funny, but in a number of large cities it is a

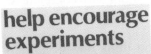

help encourage experiments

without living animals

support the Dr Hadwen Trust for Humane Research

major problem. Animals can
50 cause disease, too. It is the threat of rabies—a disease with no known cure—that has made the English government impose strict restrictions on animals
55 coming into the United Kingdom. When the Spanish government recently destroyed a number of stray dogs as protection against the same threat, English
60 tourists immediately wrote letters to the newspapers complaining about 'mass murder'.

Another problem is the carelessness of some pet owners.
65 Most little children want a dog or a cat, and they continually pester their mothers and fathers until they get one. It is only when the 'sweet little thing' has
70 been brought home that the parents realise how much time and money must be spent on 'Rover' or 'Bonzo'. At this point many of them abandon
75 it. This brings me to my last point. Pets which are allowed to run free are often not sweet at all. English farmers lose hundreds of sheep a year, killed by
80 someone's pet poodle or dachshund, and you must have read of children being mauled by pet alsations or even tigers.

You may think that I dislike
85 all pets, but this is not true at all. I would only suggest that we have got our priorities wrong and that something should be done about it. For example, the
90 authorities clearly have a responsibility to introduce stricter penalties for pet-owners whose animals savage livestock or harm little children. This
95 might deter them from being so careless. Surely it would be a good idea, too, if we made dog licences more expensive. The increased revenue from them
100 could be used for many needy causes.

As far as I'm concerned, it's time we stopped being sentimental about pets. I can see no
105 reason, for example, why we should get upset when animals are cut up for medical experiments. If this will lead us to discovering cures for serious
110 human diseases, then I say, 'keep cutting!'

We are a nation of pet-lovers. Wouldn't it be better to be lovers of human-beings?

SUGGESTIONS

A | Exercises on the text

1 VOCABULARY (K)
Find words or phrases in the text that mean:
a) scientifically collected fact or figure
b) buried
c) tiny parts of food, necessary for health
d) good for people as food
e) upset or angry about something that has happened
f) dogs which run freely
g) ask annoyingly again and again
h) badly hurt
i) order of importance
j) attack and hurt badly

2 TALKING POINTS (K)
Say whether the following statements about the text are true or false. If you think the answer is false, give your reasons.
a) Most American families seem to be more concerned about their pets than their children.
b) The writer thinks that old people usually leave their money to homes for pets when they die.
c) New York's problems amuse Julia Elliott.
d) Little children often abandon their pets.
e) Julia Elliott suggests that the authorities should give pet-owners harsher punishment if their animals cause damage.
f) Julia Elliott thinks we have stopped being sentimental about pets.
g) Julia Elliott does not feel unhappy about experiments on animals.

3 WRITING POINTS (K)
Answer the following questions with complete sentences.
a) How does Julia Elliott think money spent on pets could be better used?
b) Why does Julia Elliott think that people should not be surprised at the way American people spend money on pets?

4 CONTEXT QUESTIONS (K)
a) What does 'this' refer to in line 5?
b) What are 'they' in line 22, and what does 'as much' in line 23 refer to?
c) What is 'this' in line 29?
d) Who or what is 'it' in line 75?
e) What is it that something should be done about in lines 88/89?

5 SUMMARY WORK
a) Make a list of the four reasons the writer gives for being alarmed at the popularity of British pets.

30

SUGGESTIONS

b) Make a list of the changes the writer suggests.

c) Imagine that you are writing a report on the dangers of pets, and that in your short introduction you must briefly mention these dangers. Taking your information ONLY from the text, write the introduction in not more than 80 words.

B | Revision-test

1 Complete the blanks, and put the correct form of the words in brackets.

a) (Breathe) heavily, and (gasp) in the hot air, James climbed the steps to his bungalow.

b) James had been told that the bungalow was the perfect place (spend) the holiday ____ he took early this year.

c) It was the weather ____ made him happiest, and in fact he felt almost ____ instead of depressed as he normally did.

d) It was only right that he ____ have a holiday, because he (work) very hard that year. (8 marks)

2 Put the following into reported speech.

Teacher: I wonder if I could take Friday off. My wife's parents are arriving at Heathrow after their holiday in Greece.

Principal: I'm afraid that won't be possible. (4 marks)

3 Write sentences using the following words.

a) shop-soiled
b) to hire
c) to take part in
d) unsympathetic (4 marks)

4 Put the following words in the correct order to make sentences.

a) father/permission/him/John's/car/the/to/gave/borrow
b) girlfriend's/realised/he/driving/house/towards/his/suddenly/ wallet/had/he/forgotten/his (2 marks)

5 Write a sentence about what you could/could not do at school, using 'permission' language. (2 marks)

(Total: 20 marks)

C | Suggesting courses of action

1 Look at the following ways of making suggestions, some of which appear in the text.

SUGGESTIONS

> I would suggest *DOING*
> (Surely) it would be* a good idea if *X DID*
> Wouldn't it be† good if *X DID*
> (Surely) *X* could *DO*
> I would (only) suggest that *X* should *DO* ⟨*rather formal*⟩
> *X* clearly has the responsibility to *DO* ⟨*rather formal : strong*⟩
> It is time *X DID* ⟨*strong*⟩

* Other phrases can be used here, e.g. . . . *more sensible, advantageous.*

† Other words or phrases can be used here, e.g. *safer, sensible, more intelligent,* etc.

a. Traffic has become a major problem in most big cities. Below are some Ⓚ
suggestions for solving the problem.
  a) Surely/good idea/increase/tax on petrol
  b) I/suggest/ban cars/city centres
  c) It is time/encourage people/use public transport
  d) Surely/streets/made into pedestrian precincts
  e) It is time/ban cars/city centres
  f) Wouldn't/sensible/improve public transport
  g) The authorities/responsibility/improve public transport
  h) I/suggest/people/stop driving/work
  i) The government/responsibility/build better ring roads
  j) Surely city councils/ban cars/city centres

b. The rising crime rate in England has worried many people. Below are Ⓚ
different suggestions from different people. Form sentences by starting
with the words in brackets.
  a) More psychiatric help for criminals (The prison authorities)
  b) Prisons less comfortable (Surely)
  c) Police should be armed (I would only suggest)
  d) Bring back the death penalty (The government)
  e) Recognise that criminals – products of society (It is time)

Now complete the following in similar ways.
  f) Stricter penalties for first offenders
  g) Stop treating criminals like animals
  h) Magistrates should stop being so lenient
  i) The police force – made larger

What suggestions can you think of to help lower the crime rate?

2 In England, every houseowner pays money to the local council. This
money is called 'Rates'. On page 33 is a diagram showing how a typical
city council spent the rates in one year. The figures are in millions of
pounds.

a. Using the information, imagine that you are planning the city council's
budget for the following year. MAKE SUGGESTIONS about the amount of

SUGGESTIONS

money to be spent, and the way to spend it. In particular, MAKE SUGGESTIONS about how much should be spent on Social Services, and what exactly that money should be spent on.

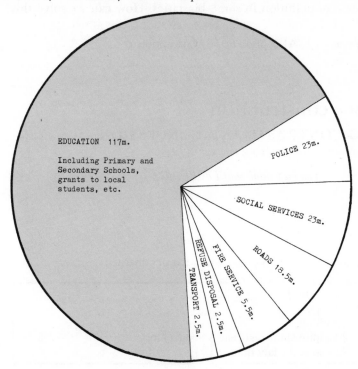

SOCIAL SERVICES include help for old people, help for children and families with problems, homes, etc., for ill and mentally disabled, day nurseries, meals taken to elderly people in their homes, etc.
TRANSPORT means subsidies to local bus companies.

b. At the end of your discussion, you should fill in the following charts.

SOCIAL SERVICES
Details of money allocated

TOTAL

BUDGET FOR THE COMING YEAR

EDUCATION

POLICE

SOCIAL SERVICES

ROADS

FIRE SERVICE

REFUSE DISPOSAL

TRANSPORT

TOTAL   £280m

SUGGESTIONS

3 Make suggestions about the following.
  a) The problem of nicotine addiction. How can we get people to stop smoking?
  b) The problem of pollution in some big cities. How can we solve this problem?

  Resources file references   1) A1 caption c)   2) G1 caption a)

D | Sentence construction

EXPRESSING CONTRASTS AND CONCESSION
Look at the following sentence from the text.

You may think that I dislike all pets
↓
BUT
↓
this is not true at all

Here are other ways of expressing the same idea of contrast.

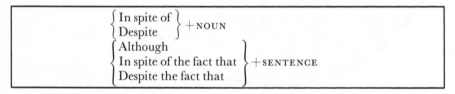

EXAMPLES
In spite of the rain he went for a walk.
{Although / In spite of the fact that} it was raining, he went for a walk.

1 Someone who read Julia Elliot's article did not completely agree with what she said. Make the following sentences which the reader might have used in her letter to the paper about the article.   Ⓚ

EXAMPLE
Elliott's point
Some old people leave their
money to dogs' homes

Reader's point
Dogs' homes are still short
of money

└──────────→ ALTHOUGH ←──────┘

Although Julia Elliott says that some old people leave their money to dogs' homes, these homes are still short of money.

Now do the same with the following.

34

SUGGESTIONS

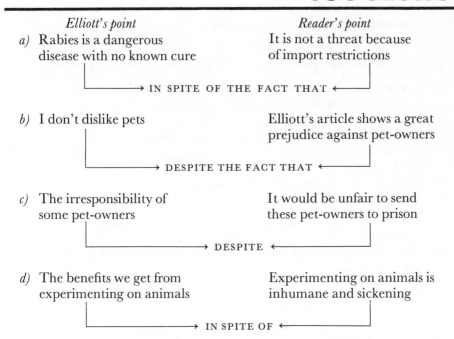

Elliott's point	Reader's point
a) Rabies is a dangerous disease with no known cure	It is not a threat because of import restrictions

IN SPITE OF THE FACT THAT

b) I don't dislike pets — Elliott's article shows a great prejudice against pet-owners

DESPITE THE FACT THAT

c) The irresponsibility of some pet-owners — It would be unfair to send these pet-owners to prison

DESPITE

d) The benefits we get from experimenting on animals — Experimenting on animals is inhumane and sickening

IN SPITE OF

2 Read the following story.

'Two months ago I bought this fridge. Very expensive it was too. But I've had nothing but trouble from it. For a start the 'COLD CONTROL' didn't work. I set it at 'medium' and it froze everything – I had to put my butter on the stove to thaw it out. I phoned the company, but nobody came. After I'd waited a week I wrote them a letter, but still nobody came. After phoning again (with no result) I went round to see them, and they sent a man round. He said he'd fixed it, but it still didn't work. The fridge has got a guarantee, but they still sent me a bill.'

Imagine that all these things happened to you, and make statements of contrast and concession which you might use in a letter to the company.

EXAMPLE
In spite of the fact that the fridge was very expensive, it has caused a lot of trouble.

E | Structure and style

FOCUS AND IDENTIFICATION

In the following sentence, the writer is trying to focus the reader's attention on one aspect – the threat of rabies.

It is the threat of rabies . . . that has made the English government impose strict restrictions . . . (1. 50–54)

SUGGESTIONS

The reader's attention is focused by the pattern

It is . . . that . . .

This is a very common pattern in both ⟨*informal*⟩ and ⟨*formal*⟩ style if we want to

either: i) focus attention on a particular point

or: ii) clarify who or what is referred to.

EXAMPLES

i) I didn't remember him until he gave his name. (NORMAL)

$\begin{cases} \text{IT WAS}n't \ until \\ \text{IT WAS} \ only \ when \end{cases}$ *he gave his name* THAT I remembered him. (FOCUS)

ii) 'Thank you for getting the work done so quickly.'

'Don't thank me; thank Gillian.' (NORMAL)

IT's Gillian $\begin{cases} (who) \\ (that)* \end{cases}$ you should thank, not me.' (CLARIFICATION)

1 Re-write the following sentences, focusing attention or clarifying the word or phrase in italics. Ⓚ

EXAMPLE

I didn't meet *Tim* on Saturday, I met Mike.

It wasn't Tim $\begin{cases} (that) \\ (who) \end{cases}$ I met on Saturday, it was Mike.

a) 'Did Martha bring her husband with her yesterday?' 'No, she came with *Sheila Lloyd.*'

b) '*Sheila* went to school with my sister.'

c) 'Didn't *her family* emigrate to Australia?'

d) 'Yes, that's right. In fact we did*n't* know *until we saw her* that she was back in this country.'

e) 'I hear she gave young David a toy koala bear.' 'No, she didn't give it to *David*, she gave it to Alan.'

f) 'She brought *this boomerang* for David.'

g) 'Any news?' 'Yes, she's married, but she'd been with us for a *couple of hours* before she told us.' (Use . . . only after a couple of hours)

h) 'Someone she met out there?' 'Well in fact she met him *in New Zealand.*'

2 Read the following Bob Dylan poem.

SIMPLE TWIST OF FATE
They sat together in the park
As the evening sky grew dark;
She looked at him and he felt a spark
Tingle to his bones.
'Twas then he felt alone
And wished that he'd gone straight
And watched out for a simple twist of fate.

* The same rules for relatives apply here as in Unit 2, SENTENCE CONSTRUCTION.

36

They walked along by the old canal
A little confused, I remember well,
And stopped into a strange hotel
With a neon burning bright.
He felt the heat of the night
Hit him like a freight train,
Moving with a simple twist of fate.

A saxophone someplace far off played
As she was walking by the arcade.
As the light burst through a beat-up shade
Where he was waking up,
She dropped a coin into a cup
Of a blind man at the gate
And forgot about a simple twist of fate.

He hears the ticking of the clocks
And walks along with a parrot that talks;
Hunts her down by the waterfront docks
Where the sailors all come in.
Maybe she'll pick him out again.
How long must he wait
One more time for a simple twist of fate?

Now correct the following statements, where necessary, using the pattern (K)
'IT WAS . . .'

EXAMPLE   A saxophone was playing nearby.
           No, it was far off that it was playing.

a) He sat with her in a park one morning.
b) He felt a spark when he looked at her.
c) They stayed at a hotel they knew.
d) The story took place on a cool evening.
e) The heat hit him like an express train.
f) She gave a blind man a 10-dollar note.
g) He walks around and talks to his parrot.
h) He hunts for her by a canal.
i) The sailors all come in at the waterfront docks.

F | Topic vocabulary

FOOD AND HEALTH

1 Below are words or phrases connected with food and drink. Find out what
  they mean, using a dictionary or any other source.
   a) a diet; to go on a diet; to be on a diet
   b) a healthy / unhealthy / varied / well-balanced / calorie-controlled + diet

SUGGESTIONS

c) paunch; to put on weight; obese; obesity
d) undernourished; well-nourished; to slim; malnutrition
e) to starve; starvation
f) harvest; to harvest; crop; yield
g) famine; drought
h) food surplus; to hoard food
i) fertilisers; pesticides
j) health foods; vegetarianism; vegetarian

2 Substitute one of the above words or phrases for the parts of the following sentences which are in italics. (K)

a) Last week Mary *stopped eating so much* because she wanted to get thinner.
b) She was *incredibly fat*, and she had been *getting fatter and fatter*.
c) She lives in a country that last year suffered a *serious food shortage*.
d) Her husband, a farmer, was recently badly affected by a *lack of water*.
e) He doesn't believe in using *chemicals which stimulate growth*.
f) He is a *person who doesn't eat meat*.

G | Writing tasks
200–250 words

1 Write a newspaper article about the growing problem of a world-wide food shortage. In the first half of the article you should state the problem, and in the second suggest ways of overcoming it. Below are some notes which might help.
The headline for the article is NO SECOND HELPING.

NOTES
Overpopulation – less food for each person
        – less land for farming
        – exhaustion of natural resources
Overconsumption (particularly rich countries)
        – less food
Pollution, environmental destruction

2 OPTION BOX

> a) Smoking, an easy way to commit suicide.
> b) People do not take enough exercise.
> c) Loneliness is the old-age pensioners' most dangerous enemy.

Resources file references   1 C1 caption b)   2 E1 caption a)

5 OBLIGATION

In the light of the case of Khalem Darubi, still awaiting the result of his appeal to the Immigration Appeal Tribunal, BERNARD FOX looks at the immigration laws of this country.

LEAVE TO ENTER

If you are a man, and the woman you want to marry is settled in the United Kingdom, you may find it extremely difficult to enter this country. The Immigration Act states:
5 Husbands and fiancés are admitted for settlement only in exceptional circumstances and must hold entry clearances for that purpose.

This is the problem Mr Darubi faces.
10 If, however, the situation had been the other way round there might have been less of a problem, for a woman whose fiancé is a man who has settled in this country will normally be given permission
15 to enter the country for three months, and she can then ask for the time limit to be removed after she has got married.

Visitors to this country are normally admitted for six months, but foreign
20 students can usually stay for one year. They must attend a 'bona fide' educational institution, and they are required to study for a minimum of fifteen hours a week on a daytime course. Prospective students
25 have to show that they can afford their studies, and that they have sufficient financial resources to support themselves while in this country.

Another exception to the six-month
30 norm is that of au pair girls, who are given 'limited leave' of two years. But in general, visitors are only admitted for half a year, and only on the understanding that they have come for pleasure, not work.
35 In order to work here the foreigner needs a work permit, which must be applied for by his prospective employer. The problem here is that the Department of Employment has the right to grant or refuse these
40 permits, and there is little that can be done

about it; it would be extremely unwise for a foreign visitor to work without a permit, since anyone doing so is liable to immediate deportation. There are some
45 exceptions to this rule, most notably people from the Common Market countries, who are entitled to work without permits, and who are often given temporary residence permits of up to five
50 years. Some other people, such as doctors, foreign journalists, authors and others, can work without permits, and foreign students are normally allowed to take part-time jobs while they are studying
55 here.

The problem with the Act is not just that some of its rules are unfair—why should Mr Darubi not be allowed into the country?—but the way it is administered,
60 and the people who administer it.

The first person a visitor to these shores meets is an immigration official, and it is he, or she, who has the power to stop him coming into the country. If this happens
65 the visitor has the right to appeal first to an Inspector, and then to the Immigration Appeal Tribunal. While the appeals are being considered, the visitor has no choice but to wait in a detention centre, some-
70 times for quite a long time. Few appeals are successful.

Critics of the law say that immigration officials treat the confused visitors badly, and appear to accept or reject them for no
75 apparent reason.

Whichever side of the political fence you are on, there seems to be an urgent need for a good look at the Act, for it causes frequent argument, and in the eyes
80 of many, real injustice.

OBLIGATION

A | Exercises on the text

1 VOCABULARY (K)
Find words or phrases in the text that mean:
a) has made his or her home in a place
b) man who has agreed to marry
c) taken away, cancelled
d) likely in the future
e) enough
f) being made to leave the country against your wishes
g) allowed by right or law
h) put into practice, organise, manage
i) thought about
j) people who disagree or dislike something

2 TALKING POINTS (K)
Say whether the following statements about the text are true or false. If you think the answer is false, give your reasons.
a) Mr Darubi wants to join his fiancée in England.
b) Women wishing to marry residents of the United Kingdom have fewer problems than men do.
c) Visitors to this country can normally stay for a year.
d) A prospective employer can give or refuse a work permit.
e) Common Market residents have problems getting a work permit.
f) Immigration officials are sometimes unfair, according to critics.
g) Immigration officials go to meet immigrants at the detention centres on the shore.

3 WRITING POINTS (K)
Answer the following questions with complete sentences.
a) What would probably happen to a non-Common Market resident if he was working without a work permit and the police found out?
b) What can visitors do to get into the country if they are refused entry?
c) What does the writer think is the problem with the law?

4 CONTEXT QUESTIONS (K)
a) 'That purpose' in line 8 refers to ...
b) 'The situation' in line 10 refers to ...
c) Who are 'they' in line 21?
d) Who is 'him' in line 63?
e) What does 'it' refer to in line 78?

5 SUMMARY WORK

a) Make a list of the four things foreigners have to do or show to be allowed to study in England.

b) Write a short dialogue (not more than 150 words) between an official at the British Embassy in your country and someone who is a national of your country and wants to study in England. Use ONLY information from the text.

B | Revision-test

1 Join the following pairs of sentences using ALTHOUGH, IN SPITE OF, etc.

a) John's intelligent.
John's lazy.

b) John lives five minutes away from his office.
John never gets to work on time.

c) John is paid a lot of money.
John does no work.

(3 marks)

2 Join the following pairs of sentences using relative clauses.

a) The man was wearing a small black hat.
I saw him.

b) The briefcase was black too.
He was carrying it.

c) A girl stopped to talk to him.
Her face was very red.

d) The conversation lasted a long time.
They had this conversation.

(4 marks)

3 Write the correct form of the words in brackets, and complete the blanks.

a) Surely it (is) a good idea if the government (ban) the sale of alcohol.

b) It's time we (realise) that alcohol is very dangerous.

c) ＿＿ is alcohol ＿＿ makes people behave so badly at football matches.

d) The government ＿＿ has the ＿＿ to punish football hooligans severely.

(8 marks)

4 Write three sentences suggesting what could be done to encourage people to stop eating too much.
You should use: suggestion language, and
food and health vocabulary (5 marks)

(Total: 20 marks)

OBLIGATION

c | Obligation

1 Look at the following sentence from the text.

> *Prospective students have to show that they can afford their studies* . . . (ll. 24–26)

'*Have to*' expresses obligation. Below is a chart showing when we use '*have to*', and when we use '*must*', '*must not*', and '*need not*'.

CONCEPT	FORM	POINTS TO NOTE
The speaker decides. A stated rule or law.	must *DO* . . .*	Obligation is imposed by the speaker, or by public signs.
Obligation the speaker knows about. A habitual obligation.	have to *DO* . . .*	Obligation is imposed by external circumstances.
Negative obligation	must not *DO* . . .	The speaker says there is no choice.
No obligation	do not have to *DO* . . .	The speaker leaves the choice open.
No obligation; the speaker decides.	need not *DO* . . .	The speaker decides that an action is not necessary or not obligatory.

The past simple tense of the forms marked (*) is HAD TO *DO* . . .

a. In the following exercise, complete the blanks with the correct form from the OBLIGATION chart above. Ⓚ

a) In his new job George ____ work very hard.

b) (Mother to son): 'You ____ finish your lunch.'

c) (Sign at Zoo): 'Visitors ____ feed the animals.'

d) (Husband to wife): 'The car's broken down. I ____ go to work by train tomorrow.'

e) (Teacher to students): 'You ____ do any homework tonight, relax and have a good time.'

f) (Student to student): 'Tomorrow's a public holiday, so we ____ go to school.'

g) (Student to student): 'I'm fed up with school; we ____ do far too much homework.'

h) Last night John missed the bus, so he ____ walk home.

i) (Son to mother): '____ go to school tomorrow?'

j) Before you can become a doctor, you ____ pass a lot of exams.

b. A newspaper THE SUNDAY STAR recently held an essay competition for adults. On page 43 are the rules of the competition.

42

laurice
Fine

presents
exclusively
the UK

Essay *Competition*

CONDITIONS OF ENTRY
—Number of words: 2,500–3,000.
—Entries may be handwritten or typewritten.
—No quoting from any source.
—Final entry date: May 24th.
—Entry is open only to adults of 25–60 years old.
—Title of essay: 'My childhood'.
—Entries may be autobiographical or fictional.
—No help or advice from other people.

Now create conversations about the competition using the language from the chart above. In the conversations people will be asking about the rules of the competition. The conversations will take place between:

i) two friends who are interested in the competition, one of whom has not read the advertisement, and

ii) the organiser of the competition and a reporter from a radio station.

EXAMPLE

Reporter: *'Can teenagers take part in the competition?'*
Organiser: *'No, entrants must be between twenty-five and sixty years old.'*

2 Look at the following sentence from the text.

> *. . . they are required to study for a minimum of fifteen hours a week on a daytime course* (ll. 22–24)

There is another way of expressing OBLIGATION. Below are further ways of expressing some different kinds of OBLIGATION.

FORM	POINTS TO NOTE
to be $\left\{\begin{array}{l}\text{obliged}\\\text{required}\end{array}\right\}$ to *DO* . . .	Expresses 'official' obligation – laws, rules, etc.
to be $\left\{\begin{array}{l}\textit{made}\\\textit{forced}\\\textit{compelled}\end{array}\right\}$ $\begin{array}{l}\text{to}DO\ldots\\\langle\textit{slightly formal}\rangle\end{array}$	Somebody else *makes* you do something.
$\left\{\begin{array}{l}\text{There is}\\X\text{ has}\end{array}\right\}$ no $\left\{\begin{array}{l}\text{alternative}\\\text{choice}\end{array}\right\}$ but to *DO* . . . There is nothing for it but to *DO* . . .	Obligation in which nothing else is possible in a certain situation.

OBLIGATION

a. Below is a list of things that you have to do when you arrive at an English airport. Change the list into statements of obligation using language from the chart.

EXAMPLE have a passport . . . *You are required to have a passport.*

Now you do the same.
a) have a smallpox vaccination certificate
b) in some cases have a visa
c) fill in an entry form
d) show your passport to the immigration official
e) go through customs
f) declare any excess spirits or cigarettes

b. Below is a list of things that happened to 'Diamond Joe', a well-known smuggler, when he last arrived at Heathrow airport. Change the list into statements about what other people made him do, using the language from the chart.
a) stop at the customs
b) open his suitcase
c) turn out his pockets
d) go to a special room
e) take off his shoes
f) give the customs officials the watches tied to his jacket
g) go to the police station
h) spend a night in jail

c. Using the list in the previous exercise, show where Diamond Joe had no choice. Use the language from the chart.

EXAMPLE
He had no alternative but to open his suitcase when the customs official stopped him.

3 Answer the following questions.
a) What do you have to do to pass a driving test in your country?
b) What laws are there in your country about driving in towns and cities (e.g. speed limits, pedestrian crossings, etc.)?
c) What laws are there in your country about drinking and driving?

Using the above information, and using the language you have studied in the text, make conversations between a reporter and
i) policemen ('What would happen if. . .?', 'What do you have to do?')
ii) drivers who have committed offences ('What happened . . .?', 'What did you have to do?')

Ask about the following things
a) the day George was stopped by the police for speeding in a built-up area
b) what a policeman has to do if he sees someone speeding
c) the law about drinking and driving

d) the day Mary's brakes failed, and she went into a tree, managing to avoid a little girl

e) the day Arthur was driving too fast through a built-up area after having drunk far too much at a party. A policeman in a patrol car saw him

f) what candidates have to do to pass a driving test

g) the day a policeman was held hostage by a bank robber

EXAMPLE

Reporter: *'Mary, when did you realise that your brakes had failed?'*

Mary: *'Well, I saw this little girl playing in the street, so I had no choice but to stop quickly . . .'*

Resources file references   1 A1 caption d)   2 C1 caption a)

D | Sentence construction

RELATIVE CLAUSES – NON-DEFINING

Non-defining clauses are different from defining clauses (see Unit 2, SENTENCE CONSTRUCTION). They give extra information about something that is already clearly defined.

Look at the following sentence from the text.

In order to work here the foreigner needs *a work permit, which* must be applied for by his prospective employer. (ll. 35–37)

The *'which'*-clause is not telling us which or what kind of work permit the writer is referring to. It is giving us more information about the work permit. Here are two more examples of non-defining relative clauses.

An exception is *people from Common Market countries, who* are   SUBJECT entitled to work without permits.

The head of the Appeal Tribunal is *David Masters, who(m)*   OBJECT the Immigrant Community respects very much.

Points to note

1 Non-defining clauses tend to be rather formal in style, and are restricted in general to writing.

2 In non-defining clauses it is *not* possible to use 'that'.

3 In non-defining clauses it is *not* possible to leave out a relative.

4 Non-defining clauses are separated from the rest of the sentence by commas.

Non-defining relatives can be summarised as follows.

People and Pets

SUBJECT	OBJECT	PREPOSITION	POSSESSIVE
who	who (whom)	PREP+whom	whose

OBLIGATION

Things

SUBJECT	OBJECT	PREPOSITION	POSSESSIVE
which	which	PREP+which	*

* Possessives are usually expressed using WHICH + HAS/HAVE

EXAMPLE *My car, which has a broken fuel-gauge, is in the garage.*

1 GENERAL KNOWLEDGE TEST   Ⓚ

In this exercise fill the space with the correct answer, then make the two sentences into one containing a non-defining relative clause.

a) _____ is the highest mountain in the world.
   It is in Nepal.
b) _____ hosted the 1976 Olympic Games.
   It is in Canada.
c) _____ are organisations representing working people.
   The first of *them* was founded in Britain.
d) _____ is well-known for the production of coffee.
   Its capital used to be Rio de Janeiro.
e) Sculptors quite often use _____ to make statues.
   It is a metal alloy.
f) _____ flows through several European capitals.
   Strauss wrote a waltz *about it*.
g) _____ has made communications much easier and quicker.
   Alexander Bell pioneered *it* over a century ago.
h) _____ was forced to resign as U.S. president in 1974.
   His behaviour in the Watergate scandal was rather dubious.

2 Make sentences with non-defining clauses, on the following subjects
a) the Beatles *b)* America *c)* karate *d)* the Eiffel Tower *e)* Beethoven *f)* the Queen

E | Structure and style

FEW: LITTLE. A FEW: A LITTLE
Look at the following sentence from the text.

Few appeals are successful. (l. 71)

Few appeals has almost the same meaning as *hardly any appeals or not many appeals*. It has a NEAR NEGATIVE MEANING.

A few appeals would be completely wrong here because it has almost the same meaning as *a small number of appeals*. It has an AFFIRMATIVE MEANING.

In the charts below, notice the difference between ⟨*normal*⟩ style and ⟨*slightly formal*⟩ style.

46

OBLIGATION

UNCOUNTABLE NOUNS*	*Negative*	*Positive*	*Comparisons*
⟨NORMAL⟩	hardly any not much	a little a bit of	not as much
⟨SLIGHTLY FORMAL⟩	(very) little	a small amount of	less

*An *uncountable noun* is something you can't count, e.g. *mayonnaise, advice, money*, etc.

COUNTABLE NOUNS†	*Negative*	*Positive*	*Comparisons*
⟨NORMAL⟩	hardly any not many	a few	not as many less
⟨SLIGHTLY FORMAL⟩	(very) few	a small number of	fewer

†Remember that a *countable noun* is something you can count, e.g. *bottle, apple, tourist*, etc.

1 In this exercise, choose the best word or phrase from the chart above. Ⓚ Remember to consider negative and positive meanings and comparisons.

> **TOURIST NUMBERS DOWN THIS YEAR!**
> Jim Crane reports his interview with Alec Knowle
> of the Tourist Development Bureau.

_(a)_ tourists are expected this year than for over six years. This was the depressing message from the Tourist Development Bureau. It seems that the present economic situation has had _(b)_ effect on the trend of British holidaymakers spending their holidays abroad.

'What's needed is _(c)_ effort by British holiday resorts to give their towns _(d)_ of character. _(e)_ real attempts at modernisation have been made since the early 60's.'

The Government have offered some help with the cost of modernisation and at the moment even _(f)_ money would be useful. Nevertheless, _(g)_ people believe that the present downward trend in popularity can be quickly reversed.

'_(h)_ and _(i)_ people are willing to risk the uncertain weather in Britain. _(j)_ can be done about the weather, of course, but much more effort could surely be put into bringing our resorts into the eighties.'

2 Using the language from the chart, make a conversation in which two people are arguing about whether or not the public should be forced to wear seat-belts by law. Speaker A thinks they should, and speaker B thinks they should not.

EXAMPLE

B might say: *A bit of common sense is far more important than a law telling us what to do!*

47

OBLIGATION

Here are some words and phrases you can use.

people	death(s)	trouble to put on
accident(s)	injury(ies)	break the law
fatal accident(s)		feel safe

F | Topic vocabulary

LIFE ABROAD

1 Below is a list of words about moving to, or living in, a foreign country. Find out what each one means, using a dictionary or any other source.
   a) visa; passport; permit; document
   b) to book a ticket; to make a reservation; to pay a deposit
   c) polio; smallpox; cholera (vaccination certificate)
   d) customs; customs hall; immigration; official (two meanings)
   e) to declare (at customs); to have something/nothing to declare
   f) to smuggle; to import
   g) to pay duty on (an article); to avoid (paying); to evade
   h) citizen; alien; foreigner; tourist; immigrant
   i) resident; native; patrial; nationality (by birth/by blood)
   j) native language; mother tongue; dialect; accent

2 Write sentences about the following using language from **1** above.
   a) Getting an airline ticket
   b) Arriving at an English airport
   c) Foreigners who live in England
   d) What happened when your friend had more than the permitted number of cigarettes at customs
   e) People in your country who are foreigners
   f) The job of an immigration official

G | Writing tasks   200–280 words

1 Write a pamphlet outlining the job of a customs officer. You should state what you think his obligations are. The pamphlet will be used to try and recruit more people into the work force of the Customs and Excise Department.

2 OPTION BOX

> *a)* A letter to an English friend saying what you don't like about the place you are studying at and detailing the things you have to do.
> *b)* The story of a man who was unfairly accused of smuggling.
> *c)* The introduction to a brochure advertising a new English Language Institute in your country, stating, among other things, what the students' obligations are.

Resources file references   1 E2 caption a)   2 G4 caption a)

GENERALISATIONS

Living in a Class House

by RICHARD MARTIN

Over the last 25 years, British society has changed a great deal—or at least many parts of it have. In some ways, however, very little has changed, particularly where attitudes are concerned. Ideas about social class—whether a person is 'working-class' or 'middle-class'—is one
5 area in which changes have been extremely slow.

In the past, the working-class—that is those people who do manual work—tended to be paid less than middle-class people, such as teachers and doctors. As a result of this and also of the fact that workers' jobs were generally much less secure, distinct differences in life-styles and attitudes
10 came into existence. The typical working man would collect his wages on Friday evening and then, it was widely believed, having given his wife her 'housekeeping', would go out and squander the rest on the 3 B's— beer, 'baccy' and betting.

The stereotype of what a middle-class man did with his money was
15 perhaps nearer the truth. He was—and still is—inclined to take a longer-term view. Not only did he regard buying a house as a top priority, but he also considered the education of his children as extremely important. Both of these provided him and his family with security. Only in very few cases did workers have the opportunity (or the education and training)
20 to make such long-term plans.

Nowadays, a great deal has changed. In a large number of cases factory workers earn as much, if not more, than their middle-class supervisors. Social security and laws to improve job-security, combined with a general rise in the standard of living since the mid-fifties, have made it less necessary
25 than before to worry about 'tomorrow'. Working-class people seem slowly to be losing the feeling of inferiority they had in the past. In fact there has been a growing tendency in the past few years for the middle-classes to feel slightly ashamed of their position.

The changes in both life-styles and attitudes are probably most easily
30 seen amongst younger people. They generally tend to share very similar tastes in music and clothes, they spend their money on having a good time, and save for holidays or longer-term plans when necessary. There seems to be much less difference than in previous generations. Nevertheless, we still have a wide gap between the well-paid (whatever the type of job they
35 may have) and the low-paid. As long as this gap exists, there will always be a possibility that new conflicts and jealousies will emerge, or rather that the old conflicts will re-appear, but between different groups.

23

from *Social Change in the 20th Century*, edited by Peter Williams.

GENERALISATIONS

A | Exercises on the text

1 VOCABULARY   Ⓚ

Find words or phrases in the text that mean:
- a) safe
- b) very clear, easily seen
- c) to spend wastefully
- d) typical picture of someone or something
- e) being not as good, not as important
- f) enjoying themselves
- g) disagreements and fights
- h) to appear slowly

2 TALKING POINTS   Ⓚ

Say whether the following statements about the text are true or false.
If you think the answer is false, give your reasons.
- a) In Britain over the last quarter century little things have changed.
- b) Differences in life-style and attitudes between middle-class people and working-class people came into existence partly because of different levels of pay.
- c) The typical working man was paid in cash.
- d) On Fridays the typical working man told his wife what was to be done at home over the next week.
- e) Owning a house and educating his children well made the typical middle-class man feel safe.
- f) In the past workers did not buy houses because they simply did not earn enough.
- g) These days people are hardly concerned at all about the near future.
- h) There are dangers for the future due to the big differences in pay between the low-paid and the well-paid.

3 WRITING POINTS   Ⓚ

Answer the following questions with complete sentences.
- a) Why did differences of life-style and attitudes emerge between the middle-class and the working-class?
- b) What were the differences in the ways middle-class men and working-class men spent their money?
- c) How has the situation changed over the last 25 years?

4 CONTEXT QUESTIONS   Ⓚ

- a) 'It' in line 2 refers to . . .
- b) 'This' in line 8 refers to . . .
- c) 'His family' in line 18 refers to . . .
- d) 'Their' in line 28 refers to . . .
- e) 'We' in line 33 refers to . . .

50

GENERALISATIONS

5 SUMMARY WORK

Using the relevant information from your answers to 3 above, write a letter (in about 100 words) partly agreeing, and partly disagreeing with the views expressed in a newspaper article entitled WE'RE ALL MIDDLE-CLASS NOW.

B | Revision-test

1 Complete the blanks with FEW, A FEW, HARDLY ANY, etc.
  a) ____ people went to Mark Sim's concert at the town hall, which was very sad.
  b) Mark is not a very popular musician, so he does ____ earn ____ money.
  c) ____ people went to Mark's concert than to the orchestral concert the week before.
  d) ____ people said they enjoyed his concert, which made him very happy.   (4 marks)

2 Join the following pairs of sentences using WHO, WHICH, etc. You must use the correct punctuation.
  a) Hamlet is a tragedy.
     It was written by William Shakespeare.
  b) An actor once played the part of Hamlet in a film.
     I know him.
  c) The play is very serious.
     It is a very long play.
  d) The king gets killed in the end.
     The king is a bad man.   (4 marks)

3 Complete the blanks in the following letter.

Dear John,
I was sorry to hear about your problem. As far as __(1)__ ____ your best __(2)__ would be to try and get a divorce. You can certainly consult me about it. I would be very pleased if you came round to my office. __(3)__ Friday morning be __(4)__?
In order to get divorced, you __(5)__ be able to prove that the break-up of your marriage is your wife's fault. This is often very difficult. The law should be changed. The government ____(6)____ a responsibility __(7)__ do something about it.
Anyway, I hope something can be done.
                    Yours sincerely,   (7 marks)

4 Using the language of OBLIGATION, write sentences about the following.
  a) A man with a gun stopped Fred in the street and told Fred to give him his money.

51

GENERALISATIONS

b) What do you have to do to obtain a passport?
c) The police stopped a man in the street and asked him to go to the Police Station.
d) A mother ordered her son to wash his hands before dinner. What did she say?
e) What do you have to do to get into university in your country?

(5 marks)
(Total: 20 marks)

c | Qualifying generalisations

When we make general statements about a subject (e.g. the weather), it is necessary to show that such generalisations are not true in every case. Below you will find a number of ways of QUALIFYING GENERALISATIONS.

1 TRUE IN MOST CASES

FORM	POINTS TO NOTE
to tend (not) to *DO* ...	This is a very common pattern in both written and spoken styles.
to have a tendency to *DO* ...	Mainly used about people, rather than things. More common in written style than in spoken style.
to be inclined to *DO* ...	This is probably more often used to make critical comments.

You can make such generalisations more exact by further qualifying them with '*sometimes*', '*often*', '*generally*', '*usually*'.

EXAMPLES
They *generally tend to share* very similar tastes in music and cloths (ll. 30–31)
Middle-class people *have a tendency to be* more individualistic.
Young people *are much more inclined to challenge* authority than in the past.

a. Make the following prompts into generalisations that are true in most cases.
  a) Doctors tend/more money/teachers
  b) Workers' children/tendency/leave school/16
  c) Working-class people/inclined/think/middle-class/snobs
  d) Middle-class/tendency/vote Conservative
  e) Labour M.P.s tend not/as well-to-do/Conservative M.P.s

b. Change these sentences into generalisations that are true in most cases.
  a) Romantic novels are written by women.
  b) Paperbacks cost less than hardback books.
  c) People prefer watching T.V. these days to listening to the radio.
  d) Art critics criticise romantic novels for being unreal.
  e) People read more magazines than books.
  f) School children think poetry is silly.

GENERALISATIONS

c. What generalisations that are true in most cases can you make about the following subjects.

a) The leisure time activities of people under 25 and over 40

b) A nationality other than your own

2 UNCERTAIN GENERALISATIONS

CONCEPT	FORM		POINTS TO NOTE
I think but I'm not sure	seem	to *DO* ... to be *DOING* ...	The Simple Infinitive *(TO DO)* is used to describe fixed habits, unchanging habits/situations
	appear	to *DO* ... to be *DOING* ...	The Continuous Infinitive *(TO BE DOING)* is used to describe changing habits/situations.
	perhaps		'Perhaps' can be placed at the beginning, middle, or end of a sentence.

EXAMPLES

Working-class people *seem slowly to be losing* the feeling of inferiority they had in the past. (ll. 25–26)

Children *appear to enjoy* primary school more than secondary school.

Parents are, *perhaps*, not strict enough with their children these days.

Perhaps, parents are not strict enough with their children these days.

Parents are not strict enough with their children these days, *perhaps*.

Look at the way the following sentences are changed into uncertain generalisations.

i) Children do not worry about class differences+SEEM/APPEAR.

Children $\left\{ \begin{array}{l} \text{SEEM} \\ \text{APPEAR} \end{array} \right\}$ NOT TO WORRY about class differences.

ii) Attitudes are changing rather slowly+SEEM/APPEAR.

Attitudes $\left\{ \begin{array}{l} \text{SEEM} \\ \text{APPEAR} \end{array} \right\}$ TO BE CHANGING rather slowly.

a. Change the following sentences in the same way. Ⓚ

a) Fat people enjoy life more than thin people+APPEAR

b) A large number of children are overweight+SEEM

c) A growing number of people are taking up yoga+APPEAR

d) The price of food is increasing very rapidly+SEEM

e) Fresh fruit and vegetables are less popular than in the past+SEEM

f) Convenience foods make life much easier for working wives+APPEAR

b. Make uncertain generalisations about the following subjects. Try to include examples that show unchanging situations and others that show changing situations.

53

GENERALISATIONS

a) Modern fashions (both women's and men's)
b) Different makes of car
c) How people change when they get old (give examples of people you know who are getting old at present)

3 PHRASES SHOWING IN HOW MANY CASES A GENERALISATION IS TRUE

a) In the vast majority of cases . . .
In a large number of cases . . .
In most cases . . .
Generally (speaking) . . .
In quite a number of cases . . . } +SENTENCE
Often/sometimes/occasionally . . .
In some cases . . .
In one or two cases . . .

b) Only in a few cases . . . } +SENTENCE
(Only) in very few cases . . . (with inversion of subject and operator)*

* For further examples involving inversion see p. 55 SENTENCE CONSTRUCTION.

The phrases in group a) usually occur at the beginning of sentences, but they can also be placed at the end, or particularly in written style, in the middle.

EXAMPLES

In the vast majority of cases, working-class children leave school at 16.
In a small number of cases middle-class children end up in factory jobs.
Only in very few cases DO people without qualifications GET technical jobs.*

4 FINAL INTEGRATED PRACTICE OF GENERALISATIONS IN SECTIONS 1–3

Recently, a social survey was carried out comparing the way of life of men of various ages in Manchester and London. Here are some of the results of the survey.

	Under 25	25–40	40–65
WEIGHT	M 59–91 kilos L 57–87 kilos	M 59–100 kilos L 59–91 kilos	M 54–100 kilos L 59–95 kilos
INCOME	M £1800–3200 L £1950–4500	£1700–7600 £1950–12000	£1800–8500 £1800–15000
OWN HOUSES	M 10% L 6%	55% 45%	45% 60%
TAKE PART IN SPORT	M 65% L 57%	35% 30%	7% 10%
TELEVISION (HRS. PER WK.)	M 5–18 L 6–15	18–26 20–24	18–30 19–30

M—Manchester   L—London

GENERALISATIONS

A very similar survey was carried out 15 years ago. Here is a selection of the results.

	Under 25	25–40	40–65
WEIGHT	M 52–89 kilos L 54–84 kilos	51–91 kilos 54–89 kilos	54–91 kilos 57–91 kilos
INCOME	M £400–1000 L £450–1300	£500–2000 £600–3000	£400–2500 £500–7000
OWN HOUSES	M 3% L 4%	18% 30%	17% 35%

Make generalisation sentences in which you

a) Compare London and Manchester now
b) Compare London (or Manchester) now with 15 years ago
c) Say how things seem to be changing

EXAMPLES

i) *Young men in London tend to weigh less than young men in Manchester, but in most cases there isn't much difference.*

ii) *More and more people seem to be buying houses.*

Resources file references B2 caption a)   F2 caption a)

D | Sentence construction

INVERSION AFTER NEGATIVE INTRODUCTIONS

Look at the following two sentences from the text. Notice the form of the verbs. Are the sentences statements or questions?

i) *Not only did he regard buying a house as a top priority, but he also . . .* (ll. 16–17)
ii) *Only in very few cases did workers have the opportunity (or the education and training) to make such long-term plans.* (ll. 18–20)

Both the sentences begin with ADVERB PHRASES having NEGATIVE IDEAS. Sentences which begin with such NEGATIVE IDEAS have inversion of the verb and subject or in other words, the negative idea phrase is followed by the QUESTION-FORM of the verb and subject.

1 Re-write these statements by placing the phrase in italics at the beginning of the statement with the question-form following. Ⓚ

EXAMPLE

He *not only* regarded buying a house as a top priority, but he also . . .
Not only DID HE REGARD buying a house as a top priority, but he also . . .

a) Some people *not only* think camping is cheaper, but they actually prefer it to hotels.
b) I have *rarely* seen so many beautiful views as I saw in the Lake District.
c) Jack had *never* had such a miserable evening *before*.

55

GENERALISATIONS

d) I was *not* able to find out the result of the test *until the following month.*

e) A lot of money is being spent *in only a few places* on research into the causes of cancer.

NOTES ON USAGE

NEGATIVE INVERSION is used in both spoken and written English. *It has the effect of emphasising what is said or written.* As spoken English has many other ways of showing emphasis, e.g. intonation and stress, NEGATIVE INVERSION tends to occur *more in written style.*

Here are some of the most common negative introductions (note that some are 'nearly negative' in meaning).

Not only . . . but also . . .	Never (before/again) . . .
Not a (single) word . . .	Neither . . .
Not a soul . . .	Nor . . .
Not until/till . . .	By no means . . .
Nowhere . . .	In none of . . .
No-one . . .	Few . . .
In no way . . .	In few cases . . .
Under no circumstances . . .	Little . . .
On no account . . .	(Only) rarely . . .
No longer . . .	Hardly ever . . .
in no (other) place/country, etc.	Hardly . . . when . . .
At no (other) time . . .	No sooner . . . than . . .

In addition, phrases qualified by 'only' are similarly subjected to inversion.

   e.g. In America you can buy many kinds of whisky,
      but ONLY in Scotland *can you* find some of the rarer kinds.

'*Hardly*' and '*no sooner*' both have 'time-meanings'.

   No sooner – as soon as, immediately
   e.g. NO SOONER *had the play finished* THAN the audience burst into applause.

   Hardly – just after
   e.g. HARDLY *had the army arrived* WHEN there was a massive explosion.

2 Make emphatic statements about the following situations using negative-inversion to show the emphasis.

a) You have just seen a film which you did not enjoy at all.

b) Name one very good thing that is only to be found in your country.

c) You once went to the wrong party and did not realise for a long time.

d) You are dissatisfied with a second-hand car/refrigerator you have bought recently.

e) You refused to help a friend in difficulty, and now you feel very bad about it.

f) You got home last night feeling very tired, but as soon as you walked in the door, the phone rang.

g) Yesterday afternoon you went walking and saw no-one. It was a very pleasant experience.

h) You have just got home from holiday. It was one of the most miserable times you have ever had because it never stopped raining.

i) You are warning a child not to leave the house without telling you.

j) A politician is making a speech promising that people will not have so many taxes any longer if he is elected.

E | Structure and style

QUALIFYING AND RE-EXPRESSING STATEMENTS

Statements can be qualified or re-expressed in a variety of ways, depending on the effect you wish to achieve.

STYLE	BY EXPLAINING OR CLARIFYING	BY GIVING EXAMPLES	BY MAKING MORE PRECISE/EXACT
⟨Normal⟩ in both spoken+written	in other words that is (to say)	for example for instance	in other words to be precise*
Rather ⟨formal⟩ spoken+written			namely
⟨Formal⟩ written (mostly technical texts)	i.e.	e.g.	viz.
	BY MAKING MORE ACCURATE	BY EMPHASISING PART	BY STRENGTHENING
⟨Normal⟩ in both spoken+written	(or) at least	particularly in particular especially	what is more (and) in fact and actually†
Rather ⟨formal⟩ in both spoken+written	(or) rather (or) better		furthermore

* *to be precise* tends to come at the end of the qualifying part of the sentence, e.g.
  Seamen, *merchant seamen to be precise*, are often very interesting people.
† *Actually* and *in fact* have very similar meanings, but are used slightly differently sometimes. *Actually* tends to be used more for strengthening NEGATIVE statements than for positive ones, e.g.

i) I met Jack's sister yesterday. In fact I met practically the whole family. (*In fact* sounds better here than *actually*.)

ii) I've never met David's brother. $\begin{Bmatrix} In\ fact \\ Actually \end{Bmatrix}$ I've never met any of his family.

(Both *in fact* and *actually* are also used to contradict opinions and information, e.g.

'It has been said that children need mothers. $\begin{Bmatrix} In\ fact \\ Actually \end{Bmatrix}$ it would be more accurate to say that mothers need children.')

GENERALISATIONS

1 Complete the spaces in the following paragraph, using appropriate words and phrases from the chart above. Ⓚ

British English and American English are different languages, ____(a)____ they are distinctly different dialects of the same language. Nevertheless, the two 'dialects' are slowly moving closer together for a variety of reasons, _(b)_ as a result of telecommunications. There has been a kind of rivalry for well over two centuries. _(c)_ this rivalry has expressed itself in 'mutual snobbishness', _(d)_ each language regarding the other as somehow 'inferior'.

Attitudes in Britain have changed a lot in the last twenty years, _(e)_ the attitudes of some people have changed. Young people, _(f)_ university students, tend to use more 'American' words than their elders. You will still find the occasional true-bred English 'bull-dog' who insists that the American language, _(g)_ the accent, has a corrupting influence. What such people do not seem to realise is that English is a living language, and _(h)_ the importation and coining of new words and phrases is absolutely essential in our ever-changing world.

FINAL NOTE

The kind of phrases given in the chart are extremely important for both spoken and written English. They are rather idiomatic, so it can be a little difficult to get used to using them. Observe when you are listening to English, or reading it when such phrases are used, and try to copy their use. DON'T BE AFRAID OF MAKING MISTAKES AT FIRST, PARTICULARLY IN YOUR WRITTEN WORK.

Resources file reference B2 caption a)

F | Topic vocabulary

HOLIDAYS AND TOURISM

1 Below are words or phrases connected with holidays and tourism. Find out what each one means, using a dictionary or any other source.
  a) holiday; vacation; long weekend; bank holiday
  b) package holiday/tour; excursion; day-trip
  c) charter flight; group booking
  d) first class; tourist class
  e) voyage; outing; sightseeing tour
  f) hospitality/hospitable; facilities; service
  g) (excellent, etc.) cuisine; cleanliness; hygiene
  h) holiday resort; ruins; the site of (historical happening)
  i) night-life; window-shopping; guided tour; view
  j) tourist attraction; shrine; monument

2 Using the language above, write sentences about holidays and tourism in the following places
  a) Florence or a city in your country

b) England
c) A resort by the sea
d) A hotel
e) A place of historical importance in your country
f) The place you would most like to go to for your next holiday

Resources file reference C3 caption b)

G | Writing tasks

250–300 words

1 You are part of a group of people preparing a guide book in English for tourists to your country. It is your job to write the General Introduction. Introduce the tourists to various aspects of life in your country, making generalisations about such things as the weather, the different regions and the habits and customs of the people in those regions.

2 OPTION BOX

a) A letter to an English-speaking friend in which you tell him/her about a country or a region that you live in. You should describe the place and the way people behave.
b) Your impressions of a foreign country.
c) An article for a newspaper about the holiday habits of people from your country.

Resources file reference E2 caption b)

19th November

35 Ashfield Crescent,
Barton,
Sussex.

Dear Mrs Hugget,

You may remember that on two occasions we have discussed the
noise your children make while practising their musical instruments.
The last time we talked about the subject you agreed to make sure
that they would stop practising in the evenings, and that they would
5 confine themselves to no more than one hour's practice a day.

You can imagine my astonishment, then, when I realised that
nothing had changed and the situation was continuing as before. It is
getting so bad now that I find it difficult to stay in the house, my
nerves are shattered, and I invent any excuse to go out for the evening
10 to be away from the squeaks and wails of your children playing their
various instruments. Much as I like music, I have had enough, and to
be frank, I am not prepared to put up with the situation any more.

I am a fairly reasonable man, and I am quite prepared to help
others when I can, but this has gone far enough. I think it's high
15 time you realised your responsibilities as a member of the community,
and I must warn you that unless you do something about the situation
I will be forced to take legal action.

I have sent a copy of this letter to my solicitor.

Yours sincerely,

R.G. Barge

R.G. BARGE

39 Ashfield Crescent,
Barton,
Sussex.

21st November

Dear Mr Barge,

I was sorry to receive your letter. I had no idea that you
20 felt so strongly on the subject, and I do apologise for any
suffering we may have caused you.

Robert, my son, plays the violin, James, the trumpet, and my
daughter Emily is an accomplished cellist. They are all
extremely dedicated, and are making excellent progress in
25 their studies. I resent your description of their efforts
as 'squeaks' and 'wails', and I find it difficult to believe
that it is having the effect on your nerves that you claim -
after all, you live two houses away.

I am extremely sorry for any unnecessary hardship you have
30 suffered on our account, but I would have thought that
children's education was more important than some minor
discomfort. Are you, Mr Barge, as reasonable as you say?

I have sent your letter, and a copy of this one, to MY
solicitor.

35 I look forward to your reply.

Yours sincerely,

A.P. Huggett

A.P. Huggett (Mrs)

PROTEST
AND COMPLAINT

A | Exercises on the text

1 VOCABULARY Ⓚ

Find the words or phrases in the text that mean:

a) to limit oneself
b) surprise
c) destroyed, exhausted
d) noises made by a mouse or a rusty gate
e) noises made by someone crying very loudly or lamenting
f) very good, at a high standard
g) very keen on something, hard working, fond of
h) feel upset, angry about
i) suffering

2 TALKING POINTS Ⓚ

Say whether the following statements about the text are true or false. If
you think the answer is false, give your reasons.

a) Mrs Huggett and Mr Barge have had two conversations about the
   Huggett family's musical activities.
b) The Huggett children are confined for one hour every day.
c) Mr Barge never stays in his house.
d) Mr Barge will do something if Mrs Huggett does something.
e) The Huggett children take their musical activities very seriously.
f) Mrs Huggett is Mr Barge's next-door neighbour.
g) Mr Barge squeaks and wails in a house two doors away while he is
   inventing musical instruments.

3 WRITING POINTS Ⓚ

Answer the following questions with complete sentences.

a) What instruments do the Huggett children play?
b) What threat did Mr Barge make?
c) How does Mrs Huggett feel about Mr Barge's complaints?

4 CONTEXT QUESTIONS Ⓚ

a) 'We' in line 1 refers to . . .
b) What does 'it' in line 7 refer to?
c) What is referred to by 'this' in line 14?
d) 'It' in line 27 refers to . . .

5 SUMMARY WORK

You are Mr Nash. Write a report on the Barge/Huggett argument for
your superior. Your report should not be more than 90 words long.

PROTEST
AND COMPLAINT

B | Revision-test

1 Make the following into GENERALISATIONS.
   a) English people ____ to drink a lot of tea.
   b) English people have ____ to like dogs.
   c) These days people seem ____ more and more alcohol. Only ____ places ____ the consumption of alcohol seem to be going down.
   d) ____ some ____ drunk people are very pleasant, but generally they ____ rather aggressive. (7 marks)

2 Change or join the following sentences, beginning with the words in capitals.
   a) The hamburgers were burnt. The chips were greasy. (NOT ONLY)
   b) Jack waited for Mary for two hours. Then he finally gave up and went home. (NOT UNTIL)
   c) You cannot hear more beautiful music than the music on gramophone records. (NOWHERE)
   d) George does not go to the cinema very often. (ONLY RARELY)
   e) Paula arrived home. The telephone rang. (NO SOONER) (5 marks)

3 Write sentences using the following words or phrases.
   a) to have nothing to declare
   b) diet
   c) charter flight (3 marks)

4 Complete the blanks and write the correct form of the words in brackets.

   a) When I asked my teacher____permission to leave the class early, he ____ to let me. I was very angry.
   b) Mr Smith's boss (give) him ____ to go for an interview last Saturday.
   c) It ____ to me that your best course would be to study harder.

(5 marks)
(Total: 20 marks)

c | Protest, complaint, and apology

1 COMPLAINING
Look at the following ways of complaining, which are taken from the text.

I have had enough of	the way+SENTENCE *X DOING* ...	⟨*quite strong*⟩
I cannot { stand bear }	the way+SENTENCE *X* any longer *X DOING* ...	⟨*very strong*⟩

a. Make the following into sentences of complaint.
   a) I/enough/the way he/always taking my cigarettes
   b) I/stand/John plays/guitar

62

PROTEST AND COMPLAINT

   c) I/not bear films about cowboys any longer
   d) I/enough/people complaining
   e) I/not stand/way people always complain all the time

b. Make statements of complaint about the following.
   a) Someone who is always late for arrangements he has made
   b) Someone who is always calling round and staying too late
   c) The noise from the road outside your house

2 PROTEST AND WARNING

Look at the following ways of expressing protest and warning which are taken from the text.

> I am not prepared to *DO* . . . any longer   ⟨*rather formal*⟩
> I will not *DO* . . . any longer
> Unless *X DOES* . . ., *Y* will *DO* . . .
> It's $\begin{Bmatrix} \text{high} \\ \text{about} \end{Bmatrix}$ time *X DID* . . .   ⟨*rather informal*⟩

a. Make the following into sentences of protest and warning.   Ⓚ
   a) I/not prepared/put up with his laziness any longer
   b) It/time he stop/lazy
   c) I/not listen/his excuses any longer
   d) Unless he mends his ways, I/sack him
   e) I/not/his rudeness any longer

b. Now make statements of protest and warning about the following.
   a) Someone who always parks their car outside your house so that you cannot get in or out of the garage
   b) Someone who is always borrowing money and 'forgetting' to give it back
   c) A factory that pollutes the local river

Resources file references   1 C3 caption a)   2 F1 caption a)

3 APOLOGISING

Look at the following ways of apologising and making excuses, some of which are taken from the text.

APOLOGIES	EXCUSES
I do apologise for *DOING* . . . I am $\begin{Bmatrix} \text{extremely} \\ \text{very} \\ \text{terribly} \end{Bmatrix}$ sorry+ SENTENCE Please accept my apologies for *DOING* . . . ⟨*formal*⟩	I had no idea+ SENTENCE I had no intention of *DOING* . . . It was $\begin{Bmatrix} \text{an accident} \\ \text{unavoidable} \end{Bmatrix}$ I did not mean to *DO* . . .⟨*informal*⟩

In the following situations apologise and/or make excuses.
   a) Your friend asked you to bring a book she wanted. You forgot.

63

PROTEST AND COMPLAINT

b) A friend thought you were going to meet him/her at a pub. You didn't go because you didn't realise that he/she expected you.
c) You borrowed someone's car and had an accident.
d) At a party you are very rude about your boss. The woman on your left tells you she is your boss's sister.
e) In a bus you lose your balance and bump into someone.

4 In the following situations one person complains, protests or warns, and the other person apologises and makes excuses. You should make the exchanges that they might use in letters on the subject.

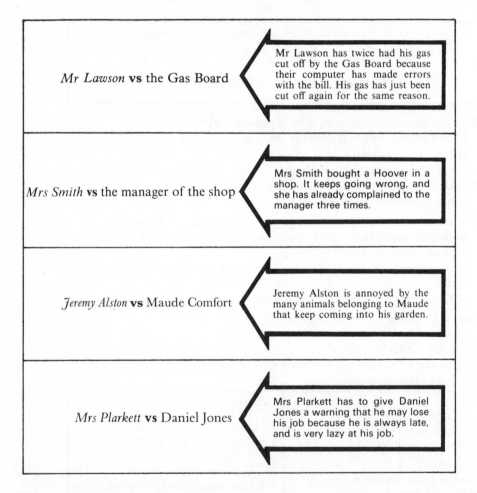

Mr Lawson **vs** the Gas Board

Mr Lawson has twice had his gas cut off by the Gas Board because their computer has made errors with the bill. His gas has just been cut off again for the same reason.

Mrs Smith **vs** the manager of the shop

Mrs Smith bought a Hoover in a shop. It keeps going wrong, and she has already complained to the manager three times.

Jeremy Alston **vs** Maude Comfort

Jeremy Alston is annoyed by the many animals belonging to Maude that keep coming into his garden.

Mrs Plarkett **vs** Daniel Jones

Mrs Plarkett has to give Daniel Jones a warning that he may lose his job because he is always late, and is very lazy at his job.

Resources file reference G1 caption b)

D | Sentence construction

CONTRAST AND CONCESSION

Look at the following sentences from the text.

Much as I like music, I have had enough . . . (l. 11)

Here are various ways of showing contrasting ideas in a sentence.

> I like music; HOWEVER, I have had enough.
> EVEN THOUGH I like music, I have had enough. ⟨*Strong*⟩
> MUCH AS I like music, I have had enough. ⟨*Strong: slightly formal*⟩
> I like music; this situation, HOWEVER, has gone far enough. ⟨*rather formal*⟩
> I like music; NEVERTHELESS, I have had enough. ⟨*rather formal*⟩

1 Join the following pairs of sentences, using the words given.   Ⓚ

a) I enjoy listening to good violin players.   I can't stand listening to people who are learning to play the violin.

EVEN THOUGH

b) I think modern composers should be encouraged.   I am not very keen on modern classical music.

MUCH AS

c) I like trumpet music.   I never enjoy horn pieces.

HOWEVER (Both forms)

d) I am very keen on classical music.   I wish my neighbours would stop playing their Beethoven symphonies so loudly on their stereo at three in the morning.

NEVERTHELESS

2 Read the following in which a woman gives her views about the modern cinema.

One of my favourite types of film is the epic, but I wish they would stop making them about terrible disasters. Most of my male friends enjoy seeing beautiful girls on the screen, but they are alarmed by the fact that most modern film makers seem to feel obliged to show so much sexual activity. I, personally, like the informal atmosphere in cinemas, but I get annoyed by people who constantly chatter, and ruin the enjoyment of

PROTEST
AND COMPLAINT

others. I like the occasional cigarette, but I find the smoke-filled atmosphere in most cinemas almost unbearable. I am not against paying for my enjoyment, but the prices they charge at most modern cinemas are ridiculous. What I'm trying to say is this: I love cinemas, but I'm going to stop going to them.

Imagine that you are the person who wrote the piece above. Using the language of contrast and concession, make sentences concerning your feelings about the cinema.

EXAMPLE *Even though I love cinemas, I'm going to stop going to them.*

3 Now make statements of CONTRAST and CONCESSION about your feelings on the following subjects.
   a) driving *b)* sun-bathing *c)* women's liberation *d)* newspapers
   e) television commercials *f)* guitars

E | Structure and style

QUITE/FAIRLY/RATHER
Look at the following sentences from the text.
 i) *I am a fairly reasonable man . . .* (l. 13)
    In this sentence you could not use *quite* or *rather* since they would change the meaning.
ii) *. . . and I am quite prepared to help others . . .* (ll. 13–14)
    In this sentence you could not use *fairly* or *rather* since they would change the meaning.

1 *Quite*
   Quite can have two different meanings.
   a) completely/extremely
   b) to a certain extent
   The meaning of *quite* often depends on the word it refers to.

EXAMPLES

Completely/extremely | To a certain extent
I'm quite sure | *The hotel was quite good*
The view was quite fantastic | *The holiday has been quite interesting*

In speech *quite* is said with a particular tone depending on its meaning.

MEANING	INTONATION
Completely/extremely	high level tone
to a certain extent	falling tone with a rising tone at the end of the phrase

The tone is very important because in some situations *quite* could have either of its meanings.

PROTEST
AND COMPLAINT

EXAMPLES   *The problem is quite easy to solve.*
This could mean *extremely easy* or *not too difficult.*

a. Using *quite* with each of the words in the list below, write sentences about
a film you recently saw.
a) interesting   *b)* original   *c)* convincing   *d)* incredible   *e)* stunning
f) horrifying   *g)* believable   *h)* tiring   *i)* moving
State whether you mean *completely/extremely* or *to a certain extent.*

b. Practise saying your sentences with the correct intonation.

2 *Fairly and Rather*

    i) FAIRLY and RATHER both qualify adjectives and adverbs, and have a
    slightly different meaning.
    FAIRLY = an ideal; it has a positive meaning
    RATHER = what you do not want; it has a negative meaning

    EXAMPLE
    It is over five weeks since the Wards were involved in a car accident,
    but Mrs Ward is still RATHER poorly, whereas Mr Ward is now
    FAIRLY well.

    ii) In comparisons, only RATHER is possible.
    Look at this example:
    However, Mrs Ward is RATHER better than she was two weeks ago.
    The man in the other car was RATHER luckier than the Wards.
    He was not even hurt.

    iii) RATHER can also mean *very much indeed.*

    EXAMPLE *Mr Ward was not quite certain whose fault the accident was, so he was*
             RATHER *relieved when the police decided not to prosecute him.*

Use FAIRLY or RATHER in the following sentences.

  a) You should be able to catch the bus ____ soon, if you leave now.
  b) This sweater looks ____ small for a child of seven. That blue one looks
     ____ bigger and it is more attractive.
  c) When Michael got top marks in his test for the third time, his teacher
     remarked that the class was ____ low for him.
  d) 'Hey! that coat suits you ____ well! I bet it was ____ expensive
     though!'
  e) 'No, in fact I got it in a sale, so it was ____ cheap, but not as cheap as
     that one you bought second-hand last week.'
  f) Understanding the difference between fairly and rather is ____
     difficult.

3 Make sentences about your work and your time at school using the
phrases given below.
a) fairly easy to learn   *b)* rather quickly   *c)* quite interesting   *d)* fairly
difficult   *e)* quite impossible   *f)* rather amusing   *g)* rather more
challenging   *h)* rather boring   *i)* quite fun

PROTEST AND COMPLAINT

F | Topic vocabulary

REACTION

1 Below are words and phrases concerned with emotional reaction. Find out their meaning, using a dictionary or any other source.
   a) amazement; surprise; astonishment
   b) horror; misery; disappointment
   c) to be appalled; to be astounded; to be disgusted
   d) ecstatic; overjoyed; thrilled
   e) to be put out; to be offended; to hurt someone's feelings
   f) furious; speechless with anger
   g) to be taken aback
   h) to be upset; to be dismayed; to be disheartened
   i) moving; touching
   j) to feel crushed; horror-stricken

2 In the following sentences complete the blanks with words from 1 above. ⓚ
   a) Last night I went to see a romantic film which was rather ____.
   b) As I came out of the cinema I saw John, who I had thought was in Australia. You can imagine my ____.
   c) I asked him how he was, and he said that he was ____. He had never felt so happy.
   d) He told me that he was going to marry Griselda, and I was completely ____. Only recently, he had told me she was horrible.
   e) When I expressed my ____ he was rather ____ because he thought I was being rude.
   f) This made me ____ because I am never rude. When he saw how angry I was, he apologised.

G | Writing tasks   200–280 words

1 Despite the fact that you have twice asked them to be quieter, your American neighbours seem to have parties every night, playing loud music, and deafening you when their friends start up their cars and motorcycles in the early morning. Write them a letter of protest and complaint.

2 OPTION BOX

> a) Recently you bought a television, which has continually gone wrong. You have complained to the manufacturers before, but nothing has been done. Write them another letter.
> b) A letter to an Australian friend in which you tell the story of an evening you spent with somebody you disliked intensely.

Resources file references   1 A1 caption b)   2 B3 caption b)

CONTROVERSY

Pilots – a special position?

BERNARD FOX looks at the high salary pilots receive

WHEN British Airways and Air France first put their brand new Concordes into service their pilots had undergone some months of special training, just as any pilot now wishing to fly the supersonic plane must undergo a rigorous conversion course: flying Concorde is clearly not the same as flying a conventional airliner. There is, of course, nothing strange about this, for every time an airline decides to use a new aircraft, the pilots must be taught to adapt to its special needs and characteristics, and every time pilots fly new aircraft they demand new rates of pay. Many of us remember how British Airways were unable to use the new 747

until the Jumbo pilots were satisfied that they were getting adequate pay.

Both in the case of the Jumbo and the Concorde, the airlines and the pilots eventually reached an agreement, but in the future pilots will no doubt continue to press for more money every time the airlines introduce new aircraft. As in the past they can argue that new aircraft require extra skill and entail extra responsibility.

The whole question of how much pilots are paid was the subject of a television programme last week when David Yeadon interviewed an airline captain who was also an active member of the pilots' union. Throughout the interview Yeadon insisted that pilots were overpaid; he even said that they were in a position to force the airlines to pay them whatever they wanted. The threat of a long strike often was enough, he said, to frighten airlines into producing the required money. The captain, naturally, argued that pilots deserved every penny they earned because of the responsibility they had, both in lives and money.

It is certainly true that the pilot's position is a special one. By any standards, the training he has to go through is unusually tough. To get an air transport pilot's licence he has to do a course that is at least as difficult as a university degree. Even then, the qualified pilot faces the constant risk of losing his licence just by failing one of the six-monthly medical and flying tests which he has to take to ensure that he is still fit, and that his flying is still up to scratch.

In most other jobs, a man reaches retiring age at sixty or sixty-five years old, but this is not the case with pilots. Their career ends in their early fifties— an age at which many other men are reaching the peak of their careers. It is difficult for a man of that age to find another job, and few pilots like the idea of being inactive so early, even if money is no problem.

The main argument against the size of pilots' salaries is that there is nothing special about the responsibilities they bear. Some people would argue that a train-driver is in the same position, and they would even go so far as to say that any bus-driver also deserves a much higher

continued on back page

CONTROVERSY

continued from front page

salary than he gets at present. It is a fact of our society that we underpay many of
75 our most important workers. People have tended to think, for example, that nurses and teachers do their jobs because they feel a special 'calling'. The argument here is that if the type of job they are
80 doing satisfies them, they don't need to be highly paid. Here it is worth pointing out that most pilots take out a loss of licence insurance, and all of them receive a pension that is equal to half their pay.
85 Whatever the rights and wrongs of the situation it is undeniable that there is something special about a pilot's job. As we live our lives down here someone is in charge of a few hundred people thirty
90 thousand feet above the Atlantic Ocean; it is not a responsibility most of us would wish. The question we should ask ourselves is how much that kind of responsibility is worth.

A | Exercises on the text

1 VOCABULARY   Ⓚ
Find words or phrases in the text that mean:
a) not out of the ordinary
b) typical things that people – or objects – have that they can be identified/recognised by
c) a sufficient amount of
d) to demand
e) specialised knowledge and expert ability
f) a very strong suggestion which can be frightening
g) very difficult
h) at the right high standard
i) the top of, summit
j) money given regularly to a person who retires

2 TALKING POINTS   Ⓚ
Say whether the following statements about the text are true or false. If you think the answer is false, give your reasons.
a) Concorde pilots need to be taught to fly Concorde even though they have flown other jets.
b) Yeadon thought that pilots were not given enough money.
c) It is difficult to get an air-pilot's licence.
d) Everybody thinks that train-drivers should get as much money as pilots.
e) Bernard Fox says that all nurses are called to become nurses.
f) Bernard Fox thinks that the job of a pilot is very ordinary.
g) Bernard Fox says that many of us would like to be pilots.

3 WRITING POINTS   Ⓚ
Answer the following questions with complete sentences.
a) How often are pilots tested to see if they are still good pilots?
b) What arguments do pilots use when they demand more pay for flying new aircraft?
c) Why does Bernard Fox think that nurses have been underpaid in the past?

70

CONTROVERSY

(K)

4 CONTEXT QUESTIONS

 a) Who exactly are 'the pilots' in line 11?
 b) Who does 'they' refer to in line 18?
 c) In line 25, who can argue that new aircraft require extra skill?
 d) Who is 'he' in line 46?
 e) Whose careers is the writer referring to in line 61?
 f) 'Them' in line 80 refers to . . .

5 SUMMARY WORK

 a) Make a list of the four main arguments from the text in favour of the high salaries of pilots.
 b) Make a list of the three main arguments from the text against the high salaries paid to pilots.
 c) Taking your information ONLY from the text write a conversation of not more than 150 words between someone who thinks that pilots are too highly paid, and someone who disagrees.

B | Revision-test

1 Complete the blanks using FAIRLY, RATHER, or QUITE.

 a) Peter's just won £1,000, and he's ____ happy.
 b) Last night's concert was ____ fantastic. I've never enjoyed myself so much!
 c) Jane Leslie's new book is ____ good, although it could have been better.
 d) I'm ____ more interested in pop music than classical music. (4 marks)

2 Make the following into PROTESTS using the words given.

 a) My neighbour plays musical instruments late at night. (NOT PREPARED)
 b) He should stop playing musical instruments at night. (HIGH TIME)
 c) He burns bonfires in his garden all the time. (HAD ENOUGH)
 d) Soon I will call the police if he does not stop playing that horrible violin. (UNLESS) (4 marks)

3 Write sentences about the following, using the words given.

 a) Pop music (EVEN THOUGH)
 b) A man who went to work with a bad cold (IN SPITE OF)
 c) Enjoying zoos, but being worried about caged animals (MUCH AS)
 d) David drives fast, but safely (HOWEVER)
 e) A rich man who is very mean (ALTHOUGH) (5 marks)

4 Write a sentence of APOLOGY for each of the following situations that happened recently.

 a) You arrived late for a dinner party.
 b) Someone asked you to pick them up and take them to the concert. You agreed but forgot. (2 marks)

71

CONTROVERSY

5 Write three sentences GENERALISING about the holiday habits of people in your country. (5 marks)

(Total : 20 marks)

c | Controversy

1 OTHER PEOPLE'S ARGUMENTS

(One of) the (main) argument(s) $\begin{Bmatrix} \text{against} \\ \text{in favour of} \end{Bmatrix}$ X is that ...
It has been $\begin{Bmatrix} \text{said} \\ \text{argued} \end{Bmatrix}$ that ...
Some people would argue that ...
It can be argued that ...

NOTE The writer may or may not agree with such arguments.

a. Jet travel – particularly with planes like the Jumbo and Concorde – has always been a controversial subject. Below are statements about it which are, or have been, other people's arguments. Use the language from the chart to make these statements as if you were writing about/discussing the subject.

  EXAMPLE   Jet aircraft are unnecessary.
  It has been said that jet aircraft are unnecessary.

Now do the same with the following.

  a) People need to get from place to place very quickly, and because of this we need jet transport.
  b) All aircraft, and particularly Concorde, are too noisy.
  c) Air travel helps to bring countries closer together.
  d) Concorde should be banned.
  e) Jets make a lot of people's lives intolerable.
  f) Air transport is destroying our environment.

b. Using the language from the chart, can you give other people's arguments about
  a) the amount of money paid to pop stars
  b) learning classical languages like Latin and Greek

2 SUBJECTIVE ARGUMENTS
Look at the following sentence from the text

  ... it is undeniable that there is something special about the responsiblity they bear. (ll. 86/87)

Here Bernard Fox is telling us what HE thinks, and giving his subjective opinion as an argument.

72

Below is some of the language we can use for this.

It is a fact that* . . .
It is undeniable that* . . .
There can be no doubt that* . . .
(Personally) I would argue that . . .

(Personally) I would tend to $\begin{cases} \text{believe} \\ \text{argue} \\ \text{think} \end{cases}$ that . . . ⟨*slightly tentative/formal*⟩

The language marked * can also be used to state *objective* arguments.

a. Marriage has always been argued about! Below are statements about marriage which express different opinions. Imagine that they are your opinions, and change them into subjective arguments.

a) Society would not exist without marriage.
b) Marriage is unnecessary.
c) Marriage keeps couples together.
d) Marriage is important for the children.
e) A marriage licence is a worthless piece of paper.
f) Marriage restricts freedom.
g) A lot of married people get divorced.

b. Now give subjective arguments about one of the following.

a) smoking in public places   *b)* the effect of violence on television

3 RHETORICAL QUESTIONS

Rhetorical questions (questions to which the speaker/writer does not expect an answer) are often used in argument. Below are some ways of doing this.

How $\begin{cases} \text{often} \\ \text{many †times} \\ \text{long‡} \end{cases}$ must *X DO* . . . before *Y DOES* . . .?

---

† Other words can be used here, e.g. *people, children,* etc.
‡ Other words can be used here, e.g. *far, low,* etc.

EXAMPLES
How low must the value of the pound fall before the government does something about it?
How long must we wait before the government comes to its senses?

a. Now make the following pairs of sentences into Rhetorical Questions, using the question form given.   Ⓚ

EXAMPLE   A lot of accidents take place in factories.
Safety regulations must be introduced . . . How long
How long must accidents take place in factories before better safety regulations are introduced.

73

CONTROVERSY

Now do the same with the following.
a) People die in car accidents.
   We must force people to wear seat-belts . . . How many
b) Health standards are falling.
   We must train more doctors . . . How low
c) A lot of people die from cancer.
   We must ban smoking . . . How many
d) Earthquakes go on killing people.
   We must build safer buildings . . . How long
e) People are murdered.
   Violence on television must be stopped . . . How often

b. Now make rhetorical questions of your own about the following subjects.
a) War
b) Pollution

4 Censorship has always been a controversial subject, and below you will find arguments both in favour of it and against it. You should use CONTROVERSY language to make statements about it, and you should try to use

other people's arguments
subjective arguments
rhetorical questions

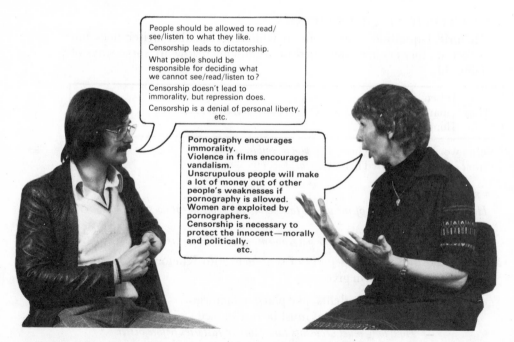

People should be allowed to read/see/listen to what they like.
Censorship leads to dictatorship.
What people should be responsible for deciding what we cannot see/read/listen to?
Censorship doesn't lead to immorality, but repression does.
Censorship is a denial of personal liberty.
etc.

Pornography encourages immorality.
Violence in films encourages vandalism.
Unscrupulous people will make a lot of money out of other people's weaknesses if pornography is allowed.
Women are exploited by pornographers.
Censorship is necessary to protect the innocent—morally and politically.
etc.

Resources file references   1 F1 caption a)   2 G5 caption a)

CONTROVERSY

D | Sentence construction

REASONS, CAUSES AND EXPLANATIONS

Look at the following sentences from the text.

> There is, of course, nothing strange about this, *for* every time an airline decides . . . (ll. 9–10)
>
> . . . . nurses and teachers do their jobs *because* they feel a special 'calling'. (ll. 76–78)

There is quite a large variety of ways in English of showing the cause of, or reason/explanation for a situation or action. The most common way in writing is to use one of the following conjunctions

    i) BECAUSE ii) AS iii) SINCE iv) FOR

In many cases, more than one of these can be used, with very little difference of meaning. However, it is important to see why they are used, and when one or other of them either should not or cannot be used.

The following two pieces of information can be connected with all four conjunctions, but with differences of meaning, and in one case a great deal of ambiguity.

    a) I went to visit my parents ACTION
    b) I was leaving the town REASON

i) *Because* EMPHASISES THE REASON, and therefore usually comes second
  I went to visit my parents because I was leaving the town.

ii) *As* CAUSES THE ACTION TO BE EMPHASISED, and so usually comes first
  As I was leaving the town, I went to visit my parents.

iii) *Since* CAUSES THE ACTION TO BE EMPHASISED, and so usually comes first
  Since I was leaving the town, I went to visit my parents.

iv) *For* has a very similar meaning to *'you see'* in spoken English. It does not give the reason for or cause of an action, it simply gives an explanation for what has just been said. For this reason, it must come after the action which it is explaining.
  I went to visit my parents, for I was leaving the town.

SINCE and AS are used in exactly the same way as each other. However, if you look at sentence (ii) above, it will be seen that the use of AS makes the sentence ambiguous. It could also mean 'at the same time'. If there is any chance of such ambiguity, SINCE must be used. SINCE also has the meaning of time, which can cause confusion too; in such cases AS must be used.

1 In the following sentences, choose which of the four conjunctions can be used in the spaces to produce unambiguous sentences. There will often be more than one possible answer. In that case say which you think is the MOST suitable.   Ⓚ

  a) _____ his wife is trying to lose some weight, she is going without lunch every day.

  b) The situation was becoming increasingly desperate, _____ night was drawing in, and we still had not found anywhere to take shelter.

c) —— he was on his way to the village, he offered to collect my groceries for me.

d) Martin has taken up fishing, —— he wants to avoid arguing so much with his mother-in-law.

e) Soon Gabriel would have to move his sheep back to the lower pastures, —— winter was drawing on, and the grass would then be blanketed in snow.

f) —— the child has disappeared, we have been unable to find out where it lives.

g) He is not in a position to give you an answer yet, —— you haven't yet made a formal offer in writing, informing him of the precise details of the deal.

h) —— George had been staying with his sister, he had not been able to see as much of Marie as he would have liked.

E | Structure and style

GERUNDS AS SUBJECTS AND OBJECTS

Look at this sentence from the text, then choose the right answer to the question which follows

Flying Concorde is clearly not the same as flying a conventional airliner. (ll. 7–8)

Is the subject of the verb *is*

a) Flying Concorde, or *b)* Concorde? (answer at the bottom of this page)*

FLYING

is like a verb. It can	is like a *noun*. It can
a) have *an object (Concorde)*	a) be the *subject of a verb*
b) be followed by *adverbs*	*(is* quicker)
(quickly/to London/at night)	b) be preceded by *adjectives*
	(good, intelligent)

Because the gerund has both the features of nouns and those of verbs, it is an excellent way of varying style, particularly written style.

1 Look at the following word groups

GERUNDS	OBJECTS	
getting married to	bank managers	*a)* HOW ADVERBS
playing	doctors	loudly/silently/slowly
allowing	donkeys	too silently
attacking	film stars	*b)* WHERE ADVERBS
riding	games	at home/in hospital/in
making	guitars	public places
shouting (at)	songs	in shops/on board ship
	suggestions	*c)* WHEN ADVERBS
		after breakfast/at night/
		once a week/on Sundays.

Begin or complete the following opinions with *meaningful gerund phrases.*
(Your sentences can be as serious or amusing as you like!)
The pattern will be as follows.

GERUND + (OBJECT) + (ADVERB group a)
　　　　　　　　　　(ADVERB groups a and b)
　　　　　　　　　　(ADVERB groups a, b and c)
　　　　　　　　　　(ADVERB groups b and c)
(Note the order of adverbs in English.)

a) I can't agree that ____ is good for health.
b) ____ tends to make you thirsty.
c) I certainly believe in ____.
d) Wouldn't you agree that ____ is an extremely relaxing way to spend a weekend?
e) ____ surely should be banned, shouldn't it?

2 Gerund phrases are particularly useful for showing our likes and dislikes.
Complete the following sentences *about yourself,* using gerund phrases.
a) One of my favourite kinds of holiday is ____.
b) ____ is something I would do more of if I had the time and the money.
c) I must say I find ____ rather boring.
d) When I was small the thing I looked forward to most was ____.
e) When I get older, I'm really going to enjoy ____.

F | Topic vocabulary

WORK

1 Here is a list of words connected with jobs and types of work. Find out
what each one means, using a dictionary or any other source.
a) dead-end
b) steady; (in)secure
c) exhausting; taxing
d) boring; tedious; soul-destroying; mechanical; frustrating
e) demanding; rewarding; useful; interesting; stimulating
f) overpaid; underpaid; badly-paid
g) manual; (un)skilled; clerical; creative
h) temporary; full-time; part-time
i) freelance; self-employed; unemployed
j) to (give the) sack; to fire; to give/hand in your notice;
to take on (an employee); to make someone redundant

2 Using words from the list above, make sentences about the following jobs
or situations.
a) working on an assembly line *b)* a barrister *c)* a research chemist *d)* a
docker *e)* a farmer *f)* a personnel officer *g)* a stockbroker *h)* a university

CONTROVERSY

lecturer *i)* a bilingual secretary *j)* an air-hostess *k)* working in the newspaper industry *l)* being a student *m)* your own job (if you have one)
Resources file reference   B3 caption a)

G | Writing tasks   250–300 words

1 Write a composition entitled SHOULD MINERS BE PAID MORE THAN NURSES?
Here are some arguments on the subject.
Miners
a) They work in appalling conditions.
b) There is a constant risk of accident.
c) Mining is an unpleasant job.
d) They work in near-darkness.
e) Coal is still a vitally important source of energy.
Nurses
a) They work very long hours.
b) Nursing is very demanding.
c) Nursing is emotionally taxing.
d) We all need nurses at some time during our lives.
e) Nurses bear a lot of responsibility.

2 OPTION BOX

a) 'The punishment should fit the crime.'
b) 'Today's pop-stars are paid far too much money.'
c) 'Marriage is dead.'

Resources file reference   G3 caption a)

HAROLD MAGNA, a freelance journalist from London, considers the relative merits of town and country.

BACK TO NATURE

FOR centuries town and country have been regarded as being in opposition to each other. It has been suggested that the superficial
5 differences between the two—wide-open spaces contrasting with brick and concrete—are less important than the contrasting attitudes of town and country.

10 I am one of the many city people who are always saying that given the choice we would prefer to live in the country away from the dirt and noise of a large city. I have managed to convince myself that if
15 it weren't for my job I would immediately head out for the open spaces and go back to

nature in some sleepy village buried in the country. But how realistic is this dream?

Cities can be frightening places. The
20 majority of the population live in massive tower blocks, noisy, squalid and impersonal. The sense of belonging to a community tends to disappear when you live fifteen floors up. All you can see from
25 your window is sky, or other blocks of flats. Children become aggressive and nervous—cooped up at home all day, with nowhere to play; their mothers feel isolated from the rest of the world. Strangely
30 enough, whereas in the past the inhabitants of one street all knew each other, nowadays people on the same floor in tower blocks don't even say hello to each other.

Country life, on the other hand, differs
35 from this kind of isolated existence in that a sense of community generally binds the inhabitants of small villages together. People have the advantage of knowing that there is always someone to turn to when
40 they need help. But country life has disadvantages too. While it is true that you may be among friends in a village, it is also true that you are cut off from the exciting and important events that take place in
45 cities. There's little possibility of going to a new show or the latest movie. Shopping becomes a major problem, and for anything slightly out of the ordinary you have to go on an expedition to the nearest large
50 town. The city-dweller who leaves for the country is often oppressed by a sense of unbearable stillness and quiet.

What, then, is the answer? The country has the advantage of peace and quiet, but
55 suffers from the disadvantage of being cut

Please turn to back page

79

CONTRAST AND COMPARISON

Continued from page 3

off: the city breeds neurosis and a feeling of isolation—constant noise batters the senses. But one of its main advantages is that you are at the centre of things, and
60 that life doesn't come to an end at half-past nine at night. Some people have found (or rather *bought*) a compromise between the two; they have expressed their preference for the 'quiet life' by leaving the
65 suburbs and moving to villages within commuting distance of the large conurbations. They generally have about as much sensitivity as the plastic flowers they leave behind—they are polluted with
70 strange ideas about change and improvement which they force on to the unwilling original inhabitants of the villages.

What then of my dreams of leaning on a cottage gate, chewing a piece of grass
75 and murmuring 'mornin'' to the locals as they pass. I'm keen on the idea, but you see there's my cat, Toby. I'm not at all sure that he would take to all that fresh air and exercise in the long grass. I mean,
80 can you see *him* mixing with all those hearty males down on the farm? No, he would rather have the electric imitation-coal fire any evening.

A | Exercises on the text

1 VOCABULARY
Find words or phrases in the text that mean:
a) only on the surface
b) dirty and unpleasant
c) enclosed in a small space
d) cut off from everything (or everyone) else
e) ties together
f) feeling weighed down by
g) a middle course
h) not real

2 TALKING POINTS
Say whether the following statements about the text are true or false. If you think the answer is false, give your reasons.
a) The writer would like to move to the country.
b) The writer will definitely move to the country.
c) The writer says that cities are dirty and noisy.
d) The writer says that people turn to others unnecessarily when they need help.
e) The writer thinks that important and exciting things happen in cities.
f) The writer says that it is a good thing that villages are cut off.
g) The writer thinks that Toby would not like the country.

3 WRITING POINTS
Answer the following questions with complete sentences.
a) In the writer's opinion what causes city people to be unhappy?
b) What do you think the writer's opinion of commuters is?
c) Do you think the writer will move to the country? Why?

CONTRAST AND COMPARISON

4 CONTEXT QUESTIONS $\quad$ (K)

  a) Who are 'we' in line 11?

  b) 'This dream' in line 18 refers to . . .

  c) What people is the writer talking about when he says 'you' in line 23?

  d) 'Its' in line 58 refers to . . .

  e) Who are 'they' in line 67?

5 SUMMARY WORK

  a) Make a list of what the writer thinks are the advantages of living in

    i) a city

    ii) the country

  b) Make a list of what the writer thinks are the disadvantages of living in

    i) a city

    ii) the country

  c) Taking your information ONLY from the text, write, in not more than 60 words, about why the country is a better place to live in than the city.

B | Revision-test

1 Complete the blanks or put the correct form of the words in brackets.

  a) One of the ____ ____ in favour of (wear) crash helmets (be) that they reduce fatal accidents.

  b) Some people ____ ____ that motorcyclists should not be forced to wear crash helmets.

  c) (Ride) motorcycles without (wear) crash helmets is (ask) for trouble.

  $\hspace{8cm}$ (7 marks)

2 Rearrange the following groups of words into grammatically accurate sentences.

  a) Unhappy/you/are/when/to/place/go/the/the/pub/is.

  b) Bad/you/is/for/too/alcohol/much/drinking/but.

  c) Britain/afternoon/close/in/have/pubs/to/at/in/the/three o'clock.

  d) Unhappy/important/three o'clock/is/be/after/not/to/it! $\quad$ (4 marks)

3 Rewrite the following sentences, focusing attention on or clarifying word or phrases in italics.

  a) Jack didn't come *on Friday*, he came on Saturday.

  b) He wasn't with *Alison*, he was with Diane.

  c) Didn't *Diane* get divorced last year? $\hspace{3cm}$ (3 marks)

4 Write three sentences on the subject of capital punishment using

        controversy language

        gerunds $\hspace{5cm}$ (6 marks)

  $\hspace{7cm}$ (Total: 20 marks)

CONTRAST AND COMPARISON

c | Advantages and disadvantages

1 DIFFERENCES

Look at the following sentence from the text:

Country life, on the other hand, *differs from* this kind of isolated existence *in that* a sense of community generally binds the inhabitants of small villages together. (ll. 34–37)

Using the pattern, *X differs from Y in that . . .*, make the following sentences about quality newspapers and popular newspapers.

NOTE   Quality – the serious national newspapers
Popular – the less serious, more pictorial newspapers, less concerned with important news.

a. *a)* Quality newspapers / differ / popular newspapers in that / have more real news   Ⓚ

b) Popular newspapers / differ / quality newspapers / that / have more pictures

c) Quality newspapers/differ/popular newspapers/treat foreign news more fully

d) Quality newspapers/differ/popular newspapers/that/carry longer and more detailed articles

e) Popular newspapers/differ/quality newspapers/contain more cartoons

f) Quality newspapers/popular newspapers/include more serious criticism of the arts

g) Quality newspapers/popular newspapers/important editorials

h) Popular newspapers/quality newspapers/less tiring to read

b. Here is another way of expressing the same idea

$\left.\begin{array}{l}\text{The main difference}\\ \text{One of the differences}\end{array}\right\}$ between X and Y is that X . . .

Using this language, express the differences between quality and popular newspapers given in **a** (above).

EXAMPLE
One of the differences between quality newspapers and popular newspapers is that quality newspapers have more real news.

c. Now make sentences of your own about differences between

a) newspapers and magazines in your own country

b) men and women

2 ADVANTAGES AND DISADVANTAGES

Look at these sentences from the text

i) The country *has the advantage of* peace and quiet, but suffers from *the disadvantage of* being cut off. (ll. 53–56)

ii) But *one of its main advantages is that* you are at the centre of things. (ll. 58–59)

CONTRAST AND COMPARISON

Now look at these ways of talking about advantages and disadvantages.

(One of) the (main) $\left\{\begin{array}{l}\text{advantages}\\\text{disadvantages}\end{array}\right\}$ of $\left\{\begin{array}{l}X\\DOING\ldots\end{array}\right\}$ is that . . .

X has the $\left\{\begin{array}{l}\text{disadvantage}\\\text{advantage}\end{array}\right\}$ of $\left\{\begin{array}{l}DOING\ldots\\Y\end{array}\right\}$ ⟨*rather formal*⟩

a. Write the following sentences about the advantages and disadvantages of having a car.   Ⓚ

a) One/disadvantages/having a car/it costs a lot to insure

b) Cars have/advantage/getting you exactly where you want to go

c) The advantage/having a car/not get wet and cold/bad weather

d) Cars/disadvantage/costing a lot of money to repair

e) Cars/advantage/speed

f) One/advantages/car/not have to depend/public transport

b. Now make more sentences of your own about the advantages and disadvantages of

a) having a dictating machine rather than a secretary

b) being a vegetarian

Resources file reference   F4 caption a)

3 CHOICE

Look at the following sentence from the text

Given the choice we would prefer to live in the country . . . (ll. 11–12)

We can say

If X had the $\left\{\begin{array}{l}\text{chance}\\\text{choice}\\\text{opportunity}\end{array}\right\}$ X would DO . . .

Given the $\left\{\begin{array}{l}\text{choice}\\\text{chance}\\\text{opportunity}\end{array}\right\}$ X would DO . . . ⟨*rather informal*⟩

4 You are looking at the possibility of renting one of the two places below.

HOUSE
Kitchen. Dining-room. Lounge. 3 bed-rooms. Bathroom. Separate W.C. Garage; garden. Pleasantly situated in unspoilt countryside 6 miles from city centre.
Price: £85.00 per month.

FLAT
Kitchen/dining-room. Lounge. 2 bed-rooms. Bathroom/W.C. Central heating. Ideally situated: 2 mins. walk from city centre.
Price: £65.00 per month.

CONTRAST AND COMPARISON

You should
  i) discuss the differences between them
 ii) discuss the advantages and disadvantages of both of them
iii) say what you would do if you were given the choice, giving your reasons

5 Make NO MORE than four sentences about each of the following.
You should
  i) discuss the differences between them
 ii) discuss the advantages and disadvantages they have
iii) say what you would do if you were given the choice

  a) Listening to records or going to concerts
  b) Going on package holidays or going on holiday on your own
  c) Going to work by bicycle or going by public transport
  d) Being married or being single

Resources file reference E4 caption a)

D | Sentence construction

WHILE AND WHEREAS
Look at the following sentences from the text

  i) . . . *whereas* in the past the inhabitants all knew each other, nowadays people on the same floor . . . don't even say hello . . . (ll. 30–33)
 ii) . . . *while* it's true that you may be . . ., it's also true that you are cut off from the exciting . . . events . . . (ll. 41–44)

While and *whereas* are both conjunctions (words used to join two halves of a sentence). They are used *to contrast two situations or actions*. They can usually be placed either *at the beginning* of the contrasted situations/actions (as in the examples above) or *between* the two contrasts.

EXAMPLE A bicycle is a very healthy way to travel,
$\begin{Bmatrix} while \\ whereas \end{Bmatrix}$ a car is a quick and comfortable way.

(There are some differences in use between the two words, because *while* can, of course, also have the meaning of 'at the same time as'. In most cases they are interchangeable, however.)

1 Below there are some 'contrast prompts', in which present-day life is contrasted with life 50 years ago. Make generalisations from these prompts using *while* or *whereas*. Ⓚ

50 YEARS AGO	NOWADAYS
a) families/rent homes . . .	majority/families/own/homes
b) 5%/work/agriculture . . .	only 3% work/land
c) only rich people/cars . . .	families/2 cars

84

d) people/abroad ...   millions/holiday/Spain/Morocco
e) children/school/14 ...   children have to/16
f) marry/late 20's ...   marry/early 20's/not bother/married at all

2 In a recent survey, men and women of various ages were asked what they considered to be their main leisure activity. Here are the results.

Activities	Single men 15–30	Single women 15–30	Married men 20–30	Married women 20–30	Men 30–50	Women 30–50
Taking part in sport	17	15	10	5	6	2
Reading	7	10	8	10	4	10
Television	21	27	22	29	24	30
Drinking	16	5	20	3	25	5
Cinema	5	6	2	4	—	—
Watching sport	22	8	18	7	17	4
Gardening	1	3	5	5	10	7
Handicrafts	3	10	10	22	11	18
Studying	3	4	1	—	—	—
Dancing	4	10	1	5	—	7
Other activities	1	2	3	10	3	17
	100%	100%	100%	100%	100%	100%

Make contrasting generalisations about people's preferences as follows:
a) Middle-aged men ... single men under 30
b) Single women ... married women
c) Single men ... married women
d) Men ... women
e) Single men under 30 ... married men under 30
f) Young women ... middle-aged women
g) Married men ... married women
h) Gardening
i) Studying
j) Men taking part in sport ... men watching sport

Resources file reference   E3 caption a)

CONTRAST AND COMPARISON

E | Structure and style

QUALIFYING AND DESCRIBING NOUNS

a) Generally speaking nouns are qualified by one or more single-word adjectives placed *before* them.

> EXAMPLE ... the *unwilling original* inhabitants of the villages. (ll. 71–72)

b) Certain adjectival phrases of two words also are placed *before* nouns. Such phrases are very often joined by hyphens.

> EXAMPLE ... *wide-open* spaces. (ll. 5–6)

c) In other circumstances adjectival phrases must be placed *after* nouns. This is especially true of phrases beginning with

  i) *past participles*   (DONE)
or ii) *present participles* (DOING)
or iii) *prepositions*   (AT, NEAR, etc.)

> EXAMPLE   Harold Magna's next article will be about a factory
> i) *run by a co-operative*
> ii) *producing refrigerators*
> iii) *near the docks.*

1 Find an example in the text of an adjectival phrase beginning with   Ⓚ
  a) a past participle (in paragraph 2.)
  b) a preposition (in lines 61–67)

2 Change the following sentences so that you make just one sentence which   Ⓚ
  contains a noun followed by at least one adjectival phrase.

  EXAMPLE In the newspapers there are a lot of interesting articles. They are written by Harold Magna.
  In the newspapers there are a lot of interesting articles written by Harold Magna.

  Now do the same with the following.
  a) Harold Magna is a freelance journalist. He works in London.
  b) Near Chelsea football stadium there is a new block of flats. Harold lives there. (Harold lives . . .)
  c) Near his parents' home there is a beautiful cottage. It was built in 1792. Harold once set his heart on it. (Harold . . .)
  d) Harold has a lot of friends. They live in the centre of London. That's the problem. (The problem is . . .)
  e) Harold is considering the idea of renting a weekend cottage. The idea was suggested by his father. The cottage is about 50 km from London.

3 Complete the following sentences using adjectival phrases beginning with
    a past participle
    a present participle
    a preposition

CONTRAST AND COMPARISON

EXAMPLE *I particularly like films* $\left\{\begin{array}{l}\textit{directed by John Ford.}\\ \textit{showing African wildlife.}\\ \textit{with lots of action.}\end{array}\right\}$

a) I'd really like to live in a house . . .
b) I've never met anyone . . .
c) Books . . . tend to interest me more than books . . .
d) Children . . . really get on my nerves.
e) Television programmes . . . are very stimulating.

F | Topic vocabulary

TOWN AND COUNTRY
Below are two lists – features of urban (town) and rural (country) life.

URBAN	RURAL
high-rise office blocks	cottages
main roads – side roads	country lanes – paths
city centre	village green
crowds	empty spaces
shopping precincts	general store
building sites	fields – meadows
semi-detached houses	hills – valleys
terraced houses	woods – forests
factories (factory-workers)	farms (farm-labourers)
vehicles	farm animals
hustle-and-bustle	peace and quiet
industry	agriculture
concrete – bricks	hedges – plants

1 Using a dictionary or any other source, find out which of the following descriptive adjectives could be applied to each of the words and phrases above.

hectic	lonely
isolated	claustrophobic
towering	tranquil
secluded	dreary
friendly	idyllic
personal	lively
dingy	sleepy
invigorating	depressing

2 Using the vocabulary lists above, think of at least 5 reasons why
a) you like or dislike urban life
b) you like or dislike rural life

CONTRAST AND COMPARISON

G | Writing tasks 300–350 words

1 An English friend of yours has written to you to ask what you think about the following situation. He has been offered a job in a large city in your country and wants to know whether you think it would be better to live in the city or in the country within easy commuting distance of his job. Write a letter to him giving your opinion.

2 OPTION BOX

> *a)* An objective view of the advantages and disadvantages of commercial television.
> *b)* A feasibility study on whether your company should open an office in a particular city.

Resources file references   1 B1 caption b)   2 F3 caption a)

PROBABILITY

A NATIONAL DISEASE?

JULIA ELLIOTT looks at television

At any time between four in the afternoon and midnight, at least ten million viewers are sure to be
5 watching television; this figure can even rise to 35 million at peak viewing hours. With such large numbers involved, there
10 are those who would maintain that television is in danger of becoming a national disease.

The average man or woman
15 spends about a third of his or her life asleep, and a further third at work. The remaining third is leisure time — mostly evenings and weekends, and it is during
20 this time that people are free to occupy themselves in any way they see fit. In our great-grand-fathers' days the choice of entertainment was strictly limited, but
25 nowadays there is an enormous variety of things to do. The vast majority of the population, though, seem to be quite content to spend their evenings goggling
30 at the box. Even when they go out, the choice of pub can be influenced by which one has a colour television; it is, in fact, the introduction of colour that
35 has prompted an enormous growth in the box's popularity, and there can be little likelihood

of this popularity diminishing in the near future. If, then, we have
40 to live with the monster, we must study its effects.

That the great boom in television's popularity is destroying 'the art of conversation' — a
45 widely-held middle-class opinion — seems to be at best irrelevant, and at worst demonstrably false. How many conversations does one hear
50 prefaced with the remarks, 'Did you see so-and-so last night? Good, wasn't it!', which suggests that television has had a beneficial rather than a detri-
55 mental effect on conversational habits; at least people have something to talk about! More

disturbing is the possible effect on people's minds and attitudes.
60 There seems to be a particular risk of television bringing a sense of unreality into all our lives.

Most people, it is probably
65 true to say, would be horrified to see someone gunned down in the street before their very eyes. The same sight repeated nightly in the comfort of one's living-
70 room tends to lose its impact. Could the same be true of news reports of violence and deaths in various parts of the world? This is almost certainly the case,
75 since the advent of television journalism has brought man's bitterest and bloodiest conflicts onto the small screen repeatedly. What worries many people is
80 that if cold-blooded murder — both acted and real — means so little, are scenes of earthquakes and other natural disasters likely to have much effect either?
85 Such questions are, to a large extent, unanswerable, and it is true to say that predictions about people's probable re-actions are dangerous and often
90 misleading. But if television *is* dulling our reactions to violence and tragedy, it can also be said to be broadening people's horizons by introducing them to
95 new ideas and activities — ideas which may eventually lead them into new hobbies and pastimes. In the last few years there has been a vast increase in educative
100 programmes, from the more serious Open University, to Yoga and the joys of amateur gardening. Already, then people have a lot to thank the small
105 screen for, and in all probability the future will see many more grateful viewers who have discovered new pursuits through the telly's inventive genius.
110 Television, arguably the most important invention of the twentieth century, is bound to be exerting a major influence in the life of the modern man for
115 as long as one dare predict; that it will also continue to grow in popularity as the years go by is virtually certain. Yet in arousing hitherto unknown in-
120 terests — challenging to its own hold over the lethargic minds of its devotees — it is not inconceivable that television may be sowing the seeds of its own
125 downfall.

RMING

PROBABILITY

A | Exercises on the text

1 VOCABULARY   (K)

Find words or phrases in the text that mean:
a) the time of day when people watch television the most
b) begun, caused
c) sudden and large increase
d) immediate effect
e) the coming, the arrival of
f) the furthest point of people's imaginations
g) extreme intelligence and cleverness
h) sleepy, without energy
i) a time when people do not work

2 TALKING POINTS   (K)

Say whether the following statements about the text are true or false. If
you think the answer is false, give your reasons.
a) 35 million people watch television every day.
b) Julia Elliott says that people take 'keep-fit' classes.
c) People sometimes go and see whether a pub has colour television
   before they decide whether to spend an evening there or not.
d) Some people think that television causes diseases.
e) Julia Elliott thinks television has had a bad effect on the art of
   conversation.
f) People see men gunned down on their sitting-room carpets.
g) Julia Elliott thinks that scenes of violence on television have gradually
   less effect.
h) Julia Elliott thinks television is dull.
i) The monster practises Yoga while sowing seeds in an amateur garden.

3 WRITING POINTS   (K)

Answer the following questions with complete sentences.
a) According to Julia Elliott, how do most people spend their evenings?
b) What is the effect of continual violence on television, in Julia Elliott's
   opinion?
c) Why does Julia Elliott think that television may be 'sowing the seeds of
   its own downfall'?

4 CONTEXT QUESTIONS   (K)

a) 'Her' in line 15 refers to . . .
b) Who does 'their' refer to in line 29?
c) What is 'it' in line 52?
d) What or who does 'them' refer to in line 94?

90

PROBABILITY

5 SUMMARY WORK

a. Answer the following questions
  a) What is the beneficial effect of television mentioned in the text?
  b) What three adverse effects of television are mentioned in the text?

b. Taking your information ONLY from the text, write an anti-T.V. advertisement for the 'Anti-Television League', the aim of which is to increase membership, and ask for financial contributions. Your advertisement should not be more than 100 words.

B | Revision-test

1 Complete the blanks and put the correct form of the words in brackets.
  a) ____ the advantages of (know) another language is that you can communicate with people from other countries.
  b) English people differ ____ people who are not English ____ they drink a lot of tea.
  c) ____ the choice I (buy) a villa in the South of France.
  d) The main difference ____ the South of France and England ____ the South of France is very hot.
  e) Bicycles ____ the advantage ____ (be) cheap to run.   (11 marks)

2 Join the following sentences to make GENERALISATIONS and comparisons, using WHILE, WHEREAS, and GENERALISATIONS LANGUAGE.
  a) British cars are small.
      American cars are large.
  b) British people prefer Scotch.
      Americans prefer Bourbon.
  c) British children leave school at sixteen.
      American children leave school at nineteen.   (6 marks)

3 Complete the following with a suitable ADJECTIVAL PHRASE.
  a) I like food . . .
  b) I often read books . . .
  c) I often go to the library . . .   (3 marks)
                                        (Total: 20 marks)

C | Probability, present and future

1 Look at the following ways of expressing PROBABILITY in the present and the future, some of which are taken from the text.

PROBABILITY

ALMOST CERTAINLY	ALMOST CERTAINLY NOT
Will Be $\begin{Bmatrix} bound \\ sure \end{Bmatrix}$ to Will probably Be likely to May	Won't Be hardly likely to Be unlikely to Probably won't May not
POSSIBLY	POSSIBLY NOT

↓   ↓

DO Complete action/situation *or* *BE DOING* Incomplete action/situation

Note: *May* and *will* can both be used to refer to the present as well as the future.

EXAMPLES

i) 'What's John doing at the moment?'

'He $\begin{Bmatrix} may \\ will \end{Bmatrix}$ be having his lunch.'

ii) 'Are you free tomorrow evening?'
'*No, I'll be travelling to France.*'
'*I'm not sure, I may be having dinner with my mother.*'

a. Arthur Bessant is leaving hospital tomorrow after six months. Make the ⓚ
following sentences about what he is doing NOW, using the language from
the chart above:

a) He/feel happy . . .   will
b) He/sorry/that he is leaving . . .   probably won't
c) He/read/newspaper . . .   may
d) He/drink/whisky . . .   hardly likely

b. Write sentences about what you think your friends/family are doing now.

c. Now make statements about what *will happen* and what *will be happening* ⓚ
when Arthur Bessant leaves hospital tomorrow. (Remember to use the *BE
DOING* form for actions/situations already started and not yet complete.)

a) His wife/wait . . .   will
b) He/say thank you/nurses . . .   bound to
c) He/give present/the Sister . . .   may well
d) He/walk steadily . . .   may not
e) His wife/feel happy . . .   unlikely to
f) His wife/start arguing with him again . . .   sure to
g) His wife/tell him about her boyfriend . . .   hardly likely to
h) He/find out about her boyfriend . . . may

d. Now say what you think *will/is likely to*, etc., *happen* if he finds out about
her boyfriend.

92

PROBABILITY

e. Make predictions about yourself in five years' time. Say what you *may be doing/may do*, etc., or what you *won't be doing/won't do*, etc.
Resources file reference   G3 caption b)

2 Here are some more ways of expressing PROBABILITY in the present and future, some of which are taken from the text. The language is *more formal* than that in **1**, and is more common in written English.

ALMOST CERTAINLY	It is virtually certain that+SENTENCE ⟨*rather formal*⟩ X is virtually certain to be *DOING* . . .

POSSIBLY	In all probability+SENTENCE
	 It is within the bounds of possibility that
	    +SENTENCE ⟨*rather formal*⟩
	 It is not inconceivable that+SENTENCE ⟨*very formal*⟩
	 There can be little likelihood that+SENTENCE
	    ⟨*rather formal*⟩
	 There can be little likelihood of *X DOING* . . .

CERTAINLY NOT	There is absolutely no chance that+SENTENCE There is absolutely no chance of *X DOING* . . .

EXAMPLES (most of which could refer to PRESENT or FUTURE time, depending on the context in which they occur)
   i) *He is virtually certain to be waiting for you.*
   ii) *In all probability he will be waiting for you.*
   iii) *It is not inconceivable that he will be waiting for you.*
   iv) *There can be little likelihood of him waiting for you.*

a. Make statements of PROBABILITY about the world twenty years from now; be careful about when to use *(will) DO, (will) BE DOING*.   Ⓚ

a) Fashions/different . . .	in all probability
b) Us/drive/same types of car . . .	little likelihood
c) Man/live on Mars . . .	bounds of possibility
d) Argue about the same things as we do now . . .	virtually certain
e) Cities/look the same . . .	no chance

b. Now make your own statements about the following in twenty years, using the language from the charts in **1** and **2**.
   a) transport *b)* housing *c)* family life *d)* fashions *e)* holidays *f)* ecology and the environment

Resources file references   1 B1 caption c)   2 F4 caption b)

D | Sentence construction

WHAT AND WHICH
Look at the following sentences from the text

PROBABILITY

i) *What* worries many people is that if cold-blooded murder means so little ... (ll. 79–84)

ii) How many conversations does one hear prefaced with the remark, 'Did you see so-and-so last night? Good, wasn't it!', *which* suggests that television ... (ll. 48–56)

WHAT ⟶ the thing(s) that ...
         (*what* usually refers to the things that follow)

WHICH ⟶ this situation
         (*which* refers *back* to the situation just mentioned and often *summarises* it)

| WHAT | worries many people is | that if cold-blooded murder ... |

| How many conversations ... 'Good, wasn't it!' | , | WHICH | suggests ... |

(*Note:* WHICH *always* has a comma before it in this case.)

1 Some students recently visited a large computer firm. This is an article written for the student magazine. Insert *what* or *which*, as appropriate.   Ⓚ

(a) surprised us most when we arrived was the silence, *(b)* was not *(c)* one would expect surrounded by so many machines. The manager took us round, *(d)* was very kind of him since he was obviously a busy man – *(e)* you might think strange considering computers are supposed to make life easier. Most of the students had one or two questions to ask on *(f)* they had read before coming to the company, and all of them were deeply impressed by *(g)* the manager had to say on the subject. He knew his stuff, *(h)* was a change after some of the disastrous visits we had been on previously. When we left everyone was already satisfied that *(i)* they had come to find out, and *(j)* they had wanted to see, they had seen.

2 You have just arrived back home after an educational visit to a foreign country. Make statements using '*what-*' or '*which-*' clauses about things you saw, were told, etc. (Choose a real country, possibly one you know.)

EXAMPLES   *What I liked best was the way people were so friendly. We were allowed to see whatever we wanted, which surprised me rather.*

E | Structure and style

**'THAT' AND 'WHETHER' CLAUSES AS SUBJECTS—
⟨FORMAL⟩ STYLE**

Notice these two different ways of expressing the same idea.

i) *That it will also continue to grow in popularity* is virtually beyond question. (ll. 115–118) ⟨*very formal style*⟩

ii) It is virtually beyond question that it will continue to grow in popularity. ⟨*less formal style*⟩

In (i) the subject of the verb IS is the *whole clause* in italics beginning '*That*...'
'*Whether*' *clauses* can also be used as subjects in ⟨*formal style*⟩.

iii) *Whether television has been a good or bad invention* seems to be entirely a matter of opinion. ⟨*very formal style*⟩

iv) It seems to be entirely a matter of opinion whether television has been a good or bad invention. ⟨*less formal style*⟩

Notice the different transforms which are the origin of '*that*' clauses, and '*whether*' clauses.

v) 'It will continue to grow in popularity.' + It is virtually beyond question.

   That it will continue to grow in popularity is virtually beyond question.

vi) 'Has television been a good or bad invention?' + It is entirely a matter of opinion.

   Whether television has been a good or bad invention is entirely a matter of opinion.

1 Combine the following pairs of sentences in the same way to produce ⓚ *formal style* sentences about LIFE – PAST AND PRESENT.
   a) Did people use to be happier in the past?
      It is difficult to judge.
   b) People did not have the same opportunities.
      It is quite obvious.
   c) The standard of living has risen substantially.
      It is absolutely clear for all to see.
   d) Have people benefited from technical progress?
      It seems questionable.

2 Write sentences with THAT and WHETHER clauses as subjects on the following:
   a) The impact of television on people's leisure activities
   b) The strain of living in the middle of a busy city
   c) The usefulness (or not) of English as an international language

F | Topic vocabulary

LEISURE TIME

1 Here is a list of words and phrases describing leisure time activities. Find out what each one means, using a dictionary or any other source.

PROBABILITY

a) (to do) a hobby; a pastime; handicrafts
b) to engage in spare-time activities; to take part in something
c) to practise sport
d) reading; ski-ing (and many other gerunds for pastimes)
e) to try your hand at something
f) to attend evening classes
g) to give up a hobby; to take up a hobby
h) a $\begin{Bmatrix} \text{relaxing} \\ \text{fruitful} \\ \text{profitable} \end{Bmatrix}$ way to spend time
i) to be $\begin{Bmatrix} \text{skilled in} \\ \text{good at} \end{Bmatrix}$ doing something
j) to develop (latent) talents
k) to take (a lot of) pleasure in doing something
l) to improve; improvement
m) to benefit $\begin{Bmatrix} \text{physically} \\ \text{mentally} \\ \text{psychologically} \end{Bmatrix}$ from doing something

2 Use the vocabulary above to find out the following information from people.
a) their spare-time activities, past and present
b) where they do these spare-time activities
c) why they do these spare-time activities
d) what activities they have tried and then given up, and why.

Resources file reference   C2 caption a)

G | Writing tasks   275–350 words

1 Write a composition in which you imagine what life will be like in twenty years. The title is LIFE AND LEISURE TWENTY YEARS FROM NOW.

2 OPTION BOX

a) Computers – the consequences now and in the future.
b) The likely reactions of someone who has given up smoking.
c) My next holidays.

Resources file reference   D1 caption c)

PLANNING

LETTERS TO THE

More of your letters on the proposed 'Obscenity Act'

From Kenneth Stewart, House of Commons

Sir, I feel I must register a strong protest against the proposed new legislation concerning literary censorship, which the government is to introduce in the current

5 parliamentary session. However laudable the aims of the legislation—to cut down on the flood of pornography and violence—the use of the law to achieve these

10 aims is deplorable. Once again, we are faced with an attack on individual liberty, and the depressing admission that education has failed.

In the past ten years, we have seen a

15 growing tendency to introduce legislation to make people do what is good for them. The breathalyser to cut down on drunken driving, the enforced wearing of crash-helmets and car seat-belts are just the main

20 examples of the gradual encroachment of the law on personal liberty. Our now being told what we are and are not to read represents the greatest threat so far to all this country is said to stand for, in

25 particular the belief that it is through time and education that changes in people's attitudes can best be achieved.

Surely, it is through the education system and the mass media that people

30 should be brought to discriminate wisely between 'literature' and works which have 'a tendency to deprave and corrupt' (as the law at present describes pornography). In order to warn people of such works, our

35 aim should be to give children a better, more sensitive appreciation of the classics, translated from all languages, so that they have a yardstick against which to assess the standard of other works they come

40 across. Meanwhile the media should freely discuss new works, having no fear of expressing strong and frank opinions on works, whether good or bad, so that readers are in no doubt about what they

45 are getting for their money. This should also enable people to see the purely financial, non-artistic motives of many publishers and writers alike.

I fully sympathise with the aims of the

50 legislation. It is the means to which I take exception. Under the proposed law, a Publications Board (similar to the present Board of Film Censors) would be established, to which controversial books would

55 be referred. This plan seems designed to do no more than to intimidate publishers into avoiding publication of doubtful works. And how are the judges to be chosen? On what grounds, precisely, are

60 books to be passed or rejected? The rather sketchy answers to these questions which have so far been suggested are most disturbing, posing as they do the threat of government control over what we read.

65 Although the intention of the legislation is to clamp down on books which 'tend to undermine public morality', isn't it conceivable that such a phrase might be attached to any book considered a political

70 danger to the government of the day? This, together with the proposal that the Home Secretary should be the person responsible for appointing the members of the Publications Board, represents a major

75 threat to our entire democratic tradition, and if implemented may soon bring about a state of affairs in which we have no further rights to take away. It is just one step short of dictatorship.

80 For very many years we have been warned that our fundamental rights are slowly being eroded. Clearly the time has come to fight for freedom. Ultimately, should anyone, in spite of their education,

85 wish to read trash, they ought to be free to do so. Only by schools and the media taking on the burden of exposing cheap literature for what it is can we ever hope to both turn back the tide of immorality and

90 at the same time stem the erosion of personal rights and liberty.

I am,

Yours, etc.,
K. G. STEWART,
Member of Parliament.

(partial left-column fragments:)

door
men.
me,
man
felt
days
us he
cal-
the
asked
which
ether
nsom
get in
would
that I
. 'Feel
van,
c.
was a
been
ded to
y and
I was
needed
urprise
water,
w long
me, I
ut my
he pills,
ne have
things'.
ouldn't
d to let
undid
ed, but

carrying
thinly-
'd mind
ry firm,
anding
se. Once
make a
you can
he told
might
my

97

PLANNING

A | Exercises on the text

1 VOCABULARY   Ⓚ
Find words or phrases in the text that mean:
a) worthy of praise
b) very bad and regrettable
c) to reduce
d) to choose, see the difference between
e) to encourage people to be bad, to make people bad
f) to measure and judge
g) newspapers, T.V., etc.
h) unspoken reasons for doing something
i) to be in agreement with
j) to object to
k) method(s)
l) not detailed
m) put into action
n) gradually reduced, taken away

2 TALKING POINTS   Ⓚ
Say whether the following statements about the text are true or false. Justify your answer by quoting from the text.
a) Mr Stewart is protesting against a new law about censorship.
b) Mr Stewart disagrees with attempts to discourage pornography.
c) More and more laws are being introduced which take away people's freedom to choose.
d) Trying to change people's attitudes by introducing laws is against tradition.
e) People should be better taught to choose between good and bad literature.
f) A yardstick should be used to measure books.
g) Many publishers and writers are interested in money rather than 'art'.
h) All books would have to be referred to the Publications Board if the new law were passed.
i) The reasons for rejection of books by the Publications Board have not yet been finally and clearly decided.
j) Trash should be free if people want it.

B | Comprehension test

Answer these questions.
a) What would be achieved, according to Mr Stewart, by 'giving children a better, more sensitive appreciation of the classics'? (ll.35–36)
b) 'These aims' in lines 9/10 refer to ...

c) What, according to Mr Stewart, will happen if the present proposals become law?

d) How would the public benefit from free and frank discussion in the media of new works?

e) Who are 'they' in line 37?

f) What does Mr Stewart think is 'deplorable', and why does he think so?

g) In what way are the 'sketchy answers' (l. 61) so far suggested 'disturbing'?

h) 'They' in line 63 refers to . . .

i) What does 'this plan' in line 55 refer to?

j) How does Mr Stewart consider the proposed legislation is a threat to tradition?

k) Who is referred to by 'they' in line 85?

l) In a paragraph of *not more than 80 words*, say how Mr Stewart thinks 'the tide of immorality' could best be turned back.

c | Planning

1 PLANS

	hoping	to *DO* . . .	HOPE
X is	thinking	of *DOING* . . .	PLAN
	planning	to *DO* . . .	
	proposing	to *DO* . . .	
	intending	to *DO* . . .	INTENTION
	going	to *DO* . . .	
⟨*slightly formal*⟩ X	hopes	to *DO* . . .	HOPE
	plans	to *DO* . . .	PLAN
	intends	to *DO* . . .	INTENTION
	is	to *DO* . . .	ARRANGEMENT

PLANS THAT HAVE BEEN CHANGED

X	was thinking of *DOING* . . . ,	
	was hoping to *DO* . . . ,	
	had hoped to *DO* . . . ,	
	was planning to *DO* . . . ,	but now . . .
	had planned to *DO* . . . ,	
	was proposing to *DO* . . . ,	
	had proposed to *DO* . . . ,	
	was intending to *DO* . . . ,	

PLANNING

X	had intended to *DO* . . . , was going to *DO* . . . , was to have *DONE* . . . ,	but now . . .

NOTE All these forms can refer to plans about the past or the future.

a. Below is a list of projects for a city council. You will notice that the council originally set a 'TARGET IMPLEMENTATION DATE', i.e. how long it would be before the projects could be started and finished.

Recent economic difficulties, though, have forced the council to look at their projects again, and some of them have had to be cancelled. Others have had their TARGET DATE changed.

PROJECTS	TARGET IMPLEMENTATION DATE	NEW TARGET DATES/ PROJECTS
a) Swimming-pool to be built; 50 metres.	Hopefully completed in 2 years.	*hopefully completed in 2 years-change to 25 metres.*
b) New fire-engine for town depot.	Purchase in 8 weeks.	*hopefully still possible.*
c) Subsidise arts festival.	Intention for next summer's festival.	*hopefully still possible.*
d) Purchase new Rolls-Royce for use of Mayor and other councillors.	Plan for before Christmas.	*hopefully purchase Jaguar (cheaper).*
e) Make East Street into pedestrian precinct.	Within next 6 months.	*cancelled.*
f) Build new under-pass (pedestrian) at Richmond Junction.	Arrangements completed to start construction work in four months.	*hope to arrange postponement for minimum one year.*
g) Complete ring-road.	Continue work over next year and a half.	*postponed indefinitely.*
h) Convert existing ring-road into dual carriageway, where it is single lane.	Continue work over next year and a half.	*postponed indefinitely.*
i) Implement plans for a new one-way system in the city centre.	To take effect from next June.	*intend implementation at least within next year.*
j) Employ more men in the refuse collection department.	As soon as possible.	*cancelled.*
k) Employ more clerks in the council offices.	As soon as possible.	*from next month.*

100

A secretary was at the meeting in which it was decided that certain plans had to be changed or scrapped and it is her handwriting that you can see on the Project List.

Using the language of PLANS and PLANS THAT HAVE BEEN CHANGED, make statements about the council projects. Then make statements that a *representative of the council* might make at an official press conference.

EXAMPLES

i) *The council was to have built a 50-metre swimming-pool, but now they are hoping to complete a 25-metre pool in two years.*

ii) (A representative of the council talking) *We had planned to build a 50-metre swimming-pool, but now we hope to complete a smaller 25-metre pool within the next two years.*

b. Make statements about your PLANS and your PLANS THAT HAVE BEEN CHANGED.

Make the statements about the following.

a) What you were going to be when you left school (if that is different from what you do now)

b) What you are planning to do for your next holiday

c) What you are planning/hoping to do in the next ten years

d) Something you planned that you were not able to do

2 EXPLAINING AND JUSTIFYING PLANS

The (main) $\left\{\begin{array}{l}\text{idea}\\\text{aim}\\\text{reason}\end{array}\right\}$ behind *(DOING...) X* is $\left\{\begin{array}{l}\text{that SENTENCE}\\\text{to } DO...\end{array}\right\}$

The (main) $\left\{\begin{array}{l}\text{aim of } X\\\text{reason for } DOING...\end{array}\right\}$ is $\left\{\begin{array}{l}\text{that SENTENCE}\\\text{to } DO...\end{array}\right\}$

(DOING) *X* is intended to *DO* . . .

DEFENDING PLANS

only by *DOING* . . . $\left\{\begin{array}{l}\text{can* } X \, DO...\\\text{will* } X \text{ be able to } DO...\end{array}\right\}$

* Note the inversion of subject and operator.

EXAMPLES

i) *The main reason for increasing income tax is to raise more revenue for government projects.*

ii) *The main idea behind the increase of income tax is to raise more revenue.*

iii) *Increasing income tax is intended to raise more revenue.*

iv) *Only by increasing income tax will the government be able to realise its projects.*

a. Change the following into EXPLANATIONS, JUSTIFICATIONS and DEFENCES of plans. Ⓚ

PLANNING

EXAMPLE   The Council is cleaning the local river. Then people will be able to swim in it. ONLY BY
Only by cleaning the local river will people be able to swim in it.

   a) The council is closing down one school. The council will save money. (ONLY BY)

   b) The bus timetable has been changed. The company wants to make the service more efficient. (IS INTENDED)

   c) They are proposing to build an Old People's Home. They want to cater for the growing proportion of old people. (THE MAIN AIM BEHIND)

   d) The company is withdrawing this product from the market. The company wants to carry out further tests. (THE MAIN REASON FOR)

   e) The meeting is being held at 7.30. This will enable everyone to attend. (IS INTENDED)

   f) Pay them the money you owe. You will avoid prosecution. (ONLY BY)

   g) The council is intending to demolish a lot of old buildings. They want to erect new office blocks. (THE MAIN IDEA)

b. Jack Smith has been a vacuum-cleaner salesman for ten years. He is married with no children. He and his wife have become tired of their suburban life and have decided to give up their house and life-style to go and live on a commune farm out in the country.

Jack is going to write to i) his parents
                            ii) his boss

Make some of the sentences you think he would write explaining, and defending his plan.

3 Imagine that you are at a press conference in which government spokesmen are outlining plans for a new arts complex (to include theatres, exhibition halls, etc.), which will be paid for out of taxes. This replaces an earlier plan to increase government subsidies to private theatre companies, and as a result many of them will probably be forced to close.

   a) In small groups, using the language from **1** and **2** (above), imagine that you are journalists asking about the plans and government spokesman explaining/defending the plans. You can refer to the plan on page 103.

EXAMPLE

Journalist: *Could you explain why you're not going to give subsidies to private companies?*

Government representative: *We were intending to help private companies, but we have decided that only by re-allocating that money will we be able to build the new complex.*

   b) Imagine you are the journalist writing a report of the press conference.

Resources file references   1 E1 caption b)   2 E4 caption b)

102

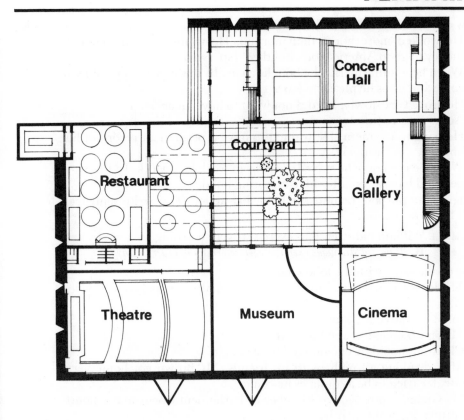

D | Sentence construction

'PURPOSE' CLAUSES

Look at the following sentences from the text

Our aim should be to give children a better, more sensitive appreciation of the classics, . . ., *so that they have a yardstick* . . . (ll. 34–38)

Meanwhile the media should freely discuss new works . . . *so that readers are in no doubt about what they are getting for their money*. (ll. 40–45)

Here are some ways of making 'purpose' clauses.

ACTION +
- so as to *DO* . . .
- so as not to *DO* . . .
- so that SENTENCE
- in order to *DO* . . . ⟨*slightly more formal*⟩

---

1 Change the following pairs of sentences into 'purpose' clauses, using the words in brackets.
   EXAMPLE He went to England. He wanted to learn English. (IN ORDER)
   He went to England in order to learn English.

103

PLANNING

Now do the same with the following.

a) He worked more hours than normal. He wanted to earn enough money to go to America for a holiday. (SO AS TO)

b) When he got to America he bought a car. In this he would be able to come and go as he pleased. (SO THAT)

c) He drove very slowly. He did not want to have an accident. (SO AS NOT TO)

d) He bought a camera. He wanted to have a permanent record of his holiday. (IN ORDER)

e) When he got home he stayed away from work for a week. In this way he could have a rest after his exhausting holiday. (SO THAT)

2 Imagine the purpose behind the following actions and write sentences with 'purpose' clauses.

EXAMPLE William did strenuous exercises every morning ...
William did strenuous exercises every morning in order to stay fit.

Now do the same with the following.

a) The local council have imposed stricter penalties for parking offences ...

b) James is studying Spanish ...

c) Mr Smith bought a gun last year ...

d) Children should be encouraged to read ...

e) After drinking all night with his friends, Mr Brown got home very late. He tried to be as quiet as he could ...

f) Mr Green, a prospective Member of Parliament, spent many hours visiting people in their homes ...

g) Maria saved money every month ...

h) The government has increased income tax ...

E | Structure and style

INVERTED CONDITIONALS

Look at the following sentence from the text

> *Should anyone*, in spite of their education, *wish to read trash*, they ought to be free to do so. (ll. 84–86)

This is another way of saying

If anyone $\left\{\begin{array}{l}\text{wishes}\\\text{should wish}\end{array}\right\}$ to read trash, they ought to be free to do so.

There are two other conditional patterns in which 'if' can be omitted by inverting the auxiliary verb and the subject

If the plan were to fail ... – *Were the plan* to fail ...

If the plan were not to succeed ... – *Were the plan not* to succeed ...

If oil had never been discovered ... – *Had oil* never been discovered ...

If oil had not been discovered ... – *Had oil not* been discovered ...

Note THE INVERSION PATTERNS ARE RATHER ⟨FORMAL⟩ IN STYLE, PARTICULARLY *(b)*

	FORM	TIME	CONCEPT
(a)	If *X* should *DO* . . . Should *X DO* . . .	Future	Unlikely, but possible that *X* will happen.
(b)	If *X* were to *DO* . . Were *X* to *DO* . . .	Future	Extremely unlikely, but theoretically possible that *X* will happen.
(c)	If *X* had *DONE* . . Had *X DONE* . . .	Past	*X* did not happen

1 Using a suitable pattern from the chart above, make 2 sentences for each ⓚ of the following prompts; in one sentence use 'if', in the other omit 'if' and invert the auxiliary verb and the subject.

EXAMPLE

The price of petrol was raised last month, so car sales have dropped again.
  i) *If the price of petrol hadn't been raised, car sales would not have dropped again.*
  ii) *Had the price of petrol not been raised, car sales would not have dropped again.*

a) We did not know your phone number, so we could not contact you.

b) I do not think the T.V. repair-man will call today, but just in case he does, I can be contacted at this number.

c) There was a serious drought in parts of Africa recently. A large number of animals died of thirst.

d) The council is unlikely to approve the plan for a local arts centre, but if it does it will be a great victory for the Local Arts Campaign.

e) There seems to be very little chance of a total ban on nuclear weapons, but such a ban would make millions of people feel much safer.

f) It is highly unlikely that more money will be spent on new universities. Primary and secondary education would certainly have to be cut as a result.

g) The level of unemployment might increase further, but I do not think it will. If it does, the trade unions will demand action from the government.

h) Ben Jonson was a sixteenth-century playwright. Shakespeare lived at the same time, and so Jonson is not so famous as he deserves to be.

i) I doubt whether anything will go wrong. Let me know if it does, won't you?

2 Complete the following sentences or add a second sentence, using an inverted conditional.

a) It is unlikely that men will land on Mars before 1980, however . . .

PLANNING

b) It is virtually out of the question that cars can be totally banned from city centres; in fact ...

c) Christopher Columbus did not know the continents of America existed.

d) It is just barely possible that books will be totally replaced by taped cassettes.

e) Prices are not expected to rise by more than 10% in the next 18 months.

3 Think of some things which are either unlikely or extremely unlikely to happen to you in the future and then imagine what you would do if these things actually happened.

F | Topic vocabulary

EQUALITY AND PREJUDICE

1 Below is a list of words relating to prejudice and (in)equality. Find out what each one means, using a dictionary or any other source.

a) Race; creed/religion; colour

b) to consider $\begin{Bmatrix} \text{someone} \\ \text{oneself} \end{Bmatrix}$ as an $\begin{Bmatrix} \text{inferior} \\ \text{superior} \end{Bmatrix}$ $\begin{Bmatrix} \text{equal} \\ \text{outsider} \end{Bmatrix}$

c) to treat someone $\begin{Bmatrix} \text{badly} \\ \text{like a second class citizen} \end{Bmatrix}$

d) to enjoy equal prospects and opportunity; equality of opportunity

e) $\begin{Bmatrix} \text{conventional} \\ \text{unconventional} \end{Bmatrix}$ attitudes/beliefs

f) (un)acceptable $\begin{Bmatrix} \text{patterns} \\ \text{modes} \end{Bmatrix}$ of behaviour

g) to take a(n) $\begin{Bmatrix} \text{positive} \\ \text{negative} \\ \text{unbiased} \end{Bmatrix}$ attitude towards someone/something

h) to exploit; exploitation

i) to be prejudiced against someone; racial prejudice, religious bigotry

j) to discriminate against; $\begin{Bmatrix} \text{racial} \\ \text{sexual} \end{Bmatrix}$ discrimination

2 Substitute one of the above words or phrases for the parts of the following sentences which are in italics.   Ⓚ

a) The new sex discrimination act gives women *the same chances as men* in the field of employment.

b) Men have previously tended to *behave towards women as if they were inferior*.

c) It was only people with *unusual ideas* who thought that women should not be *taken advantage of*.

d) It is possible that a lot of men still *have unreasonable feelings* against women.

e) The new law, however, means that women cannot be *treated worse than men*.

G | Writing tasks   300–350 words

1 A group known as INTERACE has recently been set up (with some government financial help) to help immigrants integrate more into society. The group needs public contributions to finance some of its projects, so they are preparing a press release on their future aims and plans. Write the press statement explaining in the introduction what the present problems are.

2 OPTION BOX

a) You have won a lottery and now have enough money to take a year off work and enjoy yourself. Write to an English friend explaining your plans.

b) The British government have stated an intention to treble fees for overseas students at universities and colleges. Write a letter of protest.

c) You have been put in charge of security at a major international airport. In a report to your superiors, state the changes you think necessary, and justify the inconvenience and delay that they may cause.

Resources file references   1 D2 caption b)   2 E3 caption b)

KEY

UNIT 1

A 1   *a)* marketing *b)* consultancy *c)* definitive *d)* prospects *e)* vast *f)* sales-survey *g)* on your behalf *h)* dealers *i)* vital

   2   *a)* F *b)* F *c)* T *d)* F *e)* F *f)* T *g)* T *h)* F

   3   (suggested answers) *a)* Mr Farringdon wrote to MCS to ask their advice about marketing motor cycles in North Africa. *b)* MCS felt unable to answer Mr Farringdon's questions because there were such vast differences between the countries in the area. *c)* MCS advised Mr Farringdon to have an area sales survey made. *d)* MCS advised Mr Farringdon to visit the area to 'get the feel' of it.

   4   *a)* Mr Farringdon's plan to market motor cycles in North Africa. *b)* North African countries. *c)* 'This service' refers to the investigation of possible future dealers. *d)* 'Which' refers to 'getting the feel' of the countries concerned. *e)* details.

B 1   *a)* I would advise you to learn foreign languages. *b)* If you take my advice you will continue to study. *c)* I would recommend you to get a job as soon as possible. *d)* If I were you I would go to night-school to learn a profession. *e)* I would advise you to earn enough money to travel round the world. *f)* If I were you I would work in the shop with your father. *g)* If you take my advice you will get married, settle down, and have a family.

  2**a**   *a)* It would seem to me that your best course would be to tell them how you feel. *b)* From my point of view I think you should call the police. *c)* In my opinion you should throw the rubbish back. *d)* It would seem to me that your best course would be to write a letter of complaint. *e)* As far as I'm concerned the best thing you can do is take them to court. *f)* It would appear to me that your best course would be to see a lawyer. *g)* In my opinion you should sue them for damages for nervous disorder due to the continual noise.

C 1   *a)* You will get welfare money till/until you get a new job. *b)* You will be able to find work as soon as/once the economic situation has improved. *c)* Would you fill in this form while you are waiting? *d)* You can apply for help with your rent payments as soon as you have been receiving welfare money for a month. *e)* We will also help you when your children need to buy school books. *f)* Please inform us immediately you are offered a new job.

D 1   *a)* It is crazy that children should be allowed so much freedom. *b)* It is essential that children should be taught discipline. *c)* It is only natural that parents should spoil their children. *d)* It is extremely important that children should learn to share things. *e)* It is strange that no two children should learn in the same way. *f)* It is better that parents should know about the problems their children have at school. *g)* It is only right that parents should get involved in the education of their children. *h)* It is sad that some parents should consider school a waste of time.

E 2   *a)* campaign, advertisements, commercials *b)* second-hand *c)* well-made, wear out *d)* guarantee *e)* reduced, bargains *f)* worth, badly-made, last.

108

UNIT 2

A 1   *a)* capacity *b)* constituency *c)* agricultural *d)* revelations *e)* formed *f)* moral objections *g)* fete

   2   *a)* T *b)* F *c)* F *d)* T *e)* T *f)* F *g)* T

   3   (suggested answers) *a)* Mr Huntley is the Member of Parliament representing the constituency of Trebelwyn, *b)* 'Biological Warfare' is the use of dangerous germs to cause disease. *c)* A small test-tube full of germs could give the entire population of a country a fatal disease.

   4   *a)* 'Us' are the people who live in Trebelwyn and nearby. *b)* 'It' refers to the Craven Hill government research station. *c)* 'Those' are the people who do not have strong moral objections to biological warfare. *d)* 'Our families' are the families of the Action Group members.

C 1   *a)* I wonder if we could meet on Friday. *b)* Would it be possible for me to see you on Tuesday? *c)* Could you come to my house next week? *d)* I was wondering if it would be possible for you to visit us during the summer. *e)* Could we have lunch together next week? *f)* Would it be convenient for me to pay you a visit next Thursday? *g)* I wonder if Friday would be convenient for you. *h)* Could we have a drink together next Saturday?

   2   *a)* Would you like to stay with us next weekend? *b)* Would you be interested in going to the theatre next Thursday? *c)* Would you like to come to a party next Friday? *d)* Would you be interested in going hitch-hiking next summer?

D 1   *a)* The other day I bumped into an old friend of mine that/who now works in the car trade. *b)* My friend suggested going for a drink in a pub (that) he knew. *c)* The pub was a kind of cellar with old wooden tables. *d)* I was amazed at some of the stories (that) he told about the car trade. *e)* It would seem that there are a few real criminals in the trade who the police know all about, but who are very difficult to catch. *f)* Most of the criminals work in gangs whose leaders tend to prefer driving sports cars. *g)* Many of the car dealers who Jack was talking about make their money by respraying stolen cars before selling them.

E 1   *a)* It is exciting to hear that someone from our country has won a gold medal. *b)* It is hard to believe that some parents mistreat their children. *c)* It is fascinating to see how a spider spins its web. *d)* It is encouraging to see that more and more young people are going to university. *e)* It is difficult to visualise that one day people will be living on Venus.

F 2   *a)* performing *b)* comedy, auditorium *c)* jazz, live *d)* wings, act, curtain *e)* show, night-club, cabaret.

UNIT 3

A 1   *a)* meticulously *b)* groggy *c)* heartless *d)* nasty *e)* chuckling *f)* feign *g)* accomplice *h)* humiliation

   2   *a)* F *b)* T *c)* T *d)* F *e)* F *f)* T *g)* F *h)* T

   3   (suggested answers) *a)* In the evenings Myers usually took his dog for a walk. *b)* The kidnapper called James stopped Myers and asked him the way to the church hall. *c)* The bed that Myers was strapped to was in a large van. *d)* Myers was surprised that James knew so much about him.

4   a) James. b) 'Then' refers to the moment when Myers asked to be allowed to get in touch with his wife. c) 'It' refers to what the kidnappers meant to do with Myers. d) 'He' is James. e) 'Those terrible weeks' refers to Myers' weeks in captivity.

C 2a   a) We were not allowed/permitted to feed the animals. b) Anita's father allowed her to go/let her go to the cinema. c) Fred's boss gave Fred permission to take the day off to go to his sister's wedding. d) Jake was refused permission to go to his friend's sister's wedding. e) Trainers are not allowed/permitted to give their horses stimulating drugs before races.

 3   (possible answers) a) Gloria asked for permission to leave the class early. The teacher refused to let Gloria leave early. b) Fred asked if he could have his holidays in September. Fred's boss agreed to allow him to have his holidays in September. c) Paula asked to be allowed to have a permit to stay in the country for three months longer. The immigration official refused to let her stay in the country any longer unless she was a full-time student.

D 1   a) The best way to learn things is by actually doing them yourself. b) The first people to go to when you need help are your friends. c) Tensing and Hillary were the first men to climb Everest. d) Sorry I can't come earlier, but I have a lot of arrangements to make. e) One of the problems in some urban areas is that children have no parks to play in. f) Can you imagine anything so frustrating – a bottle of wine and nothing to open it with? g) There is no way to prevent the disease from spreading.

E 1   a) Having realised/Realising very early on that they were such heartless people, I did nothing to antagonise them. b) Having tried to reason with James once or twice, I gave up because it clearly had no effect whatsoever. c) Sometimes, looking at James, I realised what greed for money could do to people. d) Having been very close to death at times, I now know how much I value life. e) Having spent 14 days in captivity I am looking forward to a long rest.

F 2   (possible answers) a) good-humoured b) bad-tempered c) mean d) unselfish e) selfish f) hard-hearted g) sympathetic h) well-mannered i) strict j) cheerful.

UNIT 4

A 1   a) statistic b) laid to rest c) vitamin d) nutritious e) resentful f) stray dogs g) pester h) mauled i) priorities j) savage.
 2   a) T b) F c) F d) F e) T f) F g) T
 3   (suggested answers) a) Julia Elliott thinks that money spent on pets could be better used if it were spent on victims of starvation and poverty. b) Julia Elliott thinks that people should not be surprised at the way Americans spend their money on pets if they have seen doggy beauty parlours and dog cemeteries.
 4   a) 'This' refers to the fact that the average family in America spent more money on its pets than on its children. b) 'They' refers to pet foods, and 'as much' refers to the price of human food. c) 'This' refers to how much the British public spent on pets last year. d) 'It' refers to the family pet. e) It is our priorities being wrong that something should be done about.

110

C **1a** *a)* Surely it would be a good idea if we increased the tax on petrol. *b)* I would suggest banning/that we should ban cars from city centres. *c)* It is time we encouraged people to use public transport. *d)* Surely the streets could be made into pedestrian precincts. *e)* It is time we banned cars from city centres. *f)* Wouldn't it be sensible if we improved public transport? *g)* The authorities clearly have a responsibility to improve public transport. *h)* I would (only) suggest that people should stop driving to work. *i)* The government clearly has a responsibility to build better ring roads. *j)* Surely city councils could ban cars from city centres.

  1b (suggested answers) *a)* The prison authorities clearly have a responsibility to provide psychiatric help for criminals. *b)* Surely prisons could be made less comfortable. *c)* I would only suggest that the police should be armed. *d)* The government clearly has a responsibility to bring back the death penalty. *e)* It is time we recognised that criminals were the products of society.

D **1** *a)* In spite of the fact that Julia Elliott says that rabies is a dangerous disease with no known cure, it is not a threat because of import restrictions. *b)* Despite the fact that Julia Elliott says that she does not dislike pets, her article shows a great prejudice against pet owners. *c)* Despite the irresponsibility of some pet owners, it would be unfair to send them to prison. *d)* In spite of the benefits we get from experimenting on animals, it is inhumane and sickening.

E **1** *a)* No, it was Sheila Lloyd she came with. *b)* It was Sheila who/that went to school with my sister. *c)* Wasn't it her family who/that emigrated to Australia? *d)* It wasn't until/It was only when we saw her that we knew she was back in this country. *e)* It wasn't David (that) she gave it to, it was Alan. *f)* It was this boomerang (that) she brought for David. *g)* It was only after a couple of hours that she told us she was married. *h)* It was in New Zealand that she met him.

  2 *a)* No, it was one evening that he sat with her in a park. *b)* No, it was when she looked at him that he felt a spark. *c)* No, it was at a strange hotel that they stayed. *d)* No, it was on a hot night that the story took place. *e)* No, it was like a freight train that the heat hit him. *f)* No, it was a coin that she gave him. *g)* No, it is the parrot that talks. *h)* No, it is by the waterfront docks that he hunts for her. *i)* Yes.

F **2** *a)* went on a diet *b)* obese, putting on weight *c)* famine *d)* drought *e)* fertilisers *f)* vegetarian

UNIT 5

A **1** *a)* settled *b)* fiancé *c)* removed *d)* prospective *e)* sufficient *f)* deported *g)* entitled *h)* administer *i)* considered *j)* critics

  2 *a)* T *b)* T *c)* F *d)* F *e)* F *f)* T *g)* F

  3 (suggested answers) *a)* If a non-Common Market resident was found to be working without a permit, he would probably be deported. *b)* If they are refused entry, visitors can appeal to Inspectors or to the Immigration Appeals Tribunal. *c)* The writer thinks the law is badly administered.

  4 *a)* settlement *b)* Mr Darubi wanting to marry a woman who is settled in the

United Kingdom. *c)* 'They' are foreign students. *d)* 'Him' is a visitor to these shores. *e)* 'It' refers to the Act.

C 1a *a)* has to *b)* must *c)* must not *d)* (will) have to *e)* needn't *f)* don't have to *g)* have to. *h)* had to *i)* Do I have to *j)* have to.

D 1 *a)* Everest, which is in Nepal, is the highest mountain in the world. *b)* Montreal, which is in Canada, hosted the 1976 Olympic Games. *c)* Trade Unions, the first of which was founded in Britain, are organisations representing working people. *d)* Brazil, the capital of which used to be Rio de Janeiro, is well-known for the production of coffee. *e)* Sculptors quite often use bronze, which is a metal alloy, to make statues. *f)* The Danube, about which Strauss wrote a waltz, flows through several European capitals. *g)* The telephone, which Alexander Graham Bell pioneered over a century ago, has made communications much easier and quicker. *h)* Nixon, whose behaviour in the Watergate scandal was rather dubious, was forced to resign as U.S. president in 1974.

E 1 (suggested answers) *a)* fewer *b)* little *c)* a bit of/a little *d)* a little *e)* hardly any *f)* a small amount of *g)* (very) few *h)* less *i)* less *j)* (very) little

UNIT 6

A 1 *a)* secure *b)* distinct *c)* squander *d)* stereotype *e)* inferiority *f)* having a good time *g)* conflict *h)* emerge

2 *a)* F *b)* T *c)* T *d)* F *e)* T *f)* F *g)* F *h)* T

3 (suggested answers) *a)* Differences of lifestyle and attitudes between middle-class and working-class people emerged because working-class people were paid less than middle-class people and had less secure jobs. *b)* The typical working-class man was paid in cash and spent his money on beer, tobacco, and betting, whereas the typical middle-class man bought a house and paid for a good education for his children. *c)* The situation has changed over the last 25 years in that working-class men now generally earn as much as middle-class men and they have greater job security.

4 *a)* British society. *b)* the fact that working-class men were paid less. *c)* the family of a typical middle-class man. *d)* the middle-classes. *e)* British society.

C 1a *a)* Doctors tend to earn more money than teachers. *b)* Workers' children have a tendency to leave school at 16. *c)* Working-class people are inclined to think that middle-class people are snobs. *d)* Middle-class people have a tendency to vote Conservative. *e)* Labour M.P.s tend not to be as well-to-do as Conservative M.P.s.

2a *a)* Fat people appear to enjoy life more than thin people. *b)* A large number of children seem to be overweight. *c)* A growing number of people appear to be taking up Yoga. *d)* The price of food seems to be increasing very rapidly. *e)* Fresh fruit and vegetables seem to be less popular than in the past. *f)* Convenience foods appear to make life much easier for working wives.

D 1 *a)* Not only do some people think that camping is cheaper, but they actually prefer it to hotels. *b)* Rarely have I seen so many beautiful views as I saw in the Lake District. *c)* Never before had Jack had such a miserable evening. *d)* Not until the following month was I able to find out the result of the test.

e) In only a few places is a lot of money being spent on research into the causes of cancer.

E 1 (suggested answers) *a)* or rather *b)* especially *c)* in particular *d)* in other words *e)* at least *f)* particularly *g)* in particular *h)* what is more

UNIT 7

A 1 *a)* confine *b)* astonishment *c)* shattered *d)* squeaks *e)* wails *f)* accomplished *g)* dedicated *h)* resent *i)* hardship
  2 *a)* T *b)* F *c)* F *d)* F *e)* T *f)* F *g)* F
  3 (suggested answers) *a)* The Huggett children play the violin, the trumpet, and the 'cello. *b)* Mr Barge threatened to take legal action. *c)* Mrs Huggett feels that Mr Barge is rather unreasonable and should be more interested in children's education than minor discomfort.
  4 *a)* Mr Barge and Mrs Huggett *b)* 'It' refers to the situation. *c)* 'This' refers to the situation that Mr Barge feels strongly about. *d)* the Huggett children practising.

C 1a *a)* I have had enough of the way he is always taking my cigarettes. *b)* I cannot stand the way John plays the guitar. *c)* I cannot bear films about cowboys anymore. *d)* I have had enough of people complaining. *e)* I cannot stand the way people always complain all the time.
   2a *a)* I am not prepared to put up with his laziness any longer. *b)* It's about/high time he stopped being lazy. *c)* I will not listen to his excuses any longer. *d)* Unless he mends his ways I will sack him. *e)* I am not prepared to put up with his rudeness any longer.

D 1 *a)* Even though I enjoy listening to good violin players, I can't stand listening to people who are learning to play the violin. *b)* Much as I think modern composers should be encouraged, I am not very keen on modern classical music. *c)* I like trumpet music; however, I never enjoy horn pieces/I like trumpet music; horn pieces, however, I never enjoy. *d)* I am very keen on classical music; nevertheless, I wish my neighbours would stop playing their Beethoven symphonies so loudly on their stereo at three in the morning.

E 2 *a)* fairly *b)* rather, rather *c)* rather *d)* rather, rather *e)* fairly *f)* fairly/rather

F 2 (suggested answers) *a)* moving *b)* astonishment *c)* ecstatic *d)* taken aback *e)* surprise, upset *f)* furious

UNIT 8

A 1 *a)* conventional *b)* characteristics *c)* adequate *d)* press for *e)* skill *f)* threat *g)* tough *h)* up to scratch *i)* peak *j)* pension
  2 *a)* T *b)* F *c)* T *d)* F *e)* F *f)* F *g)* F
  3 (suggested answers) *a)* Pilots are tested every six months. *b)* When they demand more pay for flying new aircraft, pilots argue that they need extra skill and bear extra responsibility. *c)* Bernard Fox thinks that nurses have been underpaid in the past because people thought that the job they were doing satisfied them.
  4 *a)* 'The pilots' are those who work for an airline which decides to use new aircraft. *b)* 'They' refers to the Jumbo pilots. *c)* Pilots of new aircraft can argue that new aircraft require extra skill. *d)* 'He' refers to the pilot in

general. *e)* The writer is referring to the careers of those who are not pilots. *f)* Nurses and teachers.

C 3a *a)* How many people must die in car accidents before we force them to wear seat-belts? *b)* How low must health standards fall before we train more doctors? *c)* How many people must die from cancer before we ban smoking? *d)* How long must earthquakes go on killing people before we build safer buildings? *e)* How often must people be murdered before violence on television is stopped?

D 1 *a)* as/since *b)* for *c)* since *d)* because *e)* for *f)* as *g)* because *h)* as.

UNIT 9

A 1 *a)* superficial *b)* squalid *c)* cooped up *d)* isolated *e)* binds *f)* oppressed *g)* compromise *h)* imitation

2 *a)* T *b)* F *c)* T *d)* F *e)* T *f)* F *g)* T

3 (suggested answers) *a)* City people are unhappy because they feel isolated. *b)* In my opinion, the writer thinks that commuters are insensitive. *c)* I don't think the writer will move to the country because of his job.

4 *a)* 'We' are the city people who say they want to live in the country. *b)* going back to nature *c)* He is talking about the inhabitants of tower blocks. *d)* the city *e)* 'They' are the commuters.

C 1a *a)* Quality papers differ from popular newspapers in that they have more real news. *b)* Popular newspapers differ from quality newspapers in that they have more pictures. *c)* Quality newspapers differ from popular newspapers in that they carry longer and more detailed articles. *d)* Quality newspapers differ from popular newspapers in that they treat foreign news more fully. *e)* Popular newspapers differ from quality newspapers in that they contain more cartoons. *f)* Quality newspapers differ from popular newspapers in that they include more serious criticism of the arts. *g)* Quality newspapers differ from popular newspapers in that they have more important editorials. *h)* Popular newspapers differ from quality newspapers in that they are less tiring to read.

2a *a)* One of the disadvantages of having a car is that it costs a lot to insure. *b)* Cars have the advantage of getting you exactly where you want to go. *c)* The advantage of having a car is that you don't get wet and cold in bad weather. *d)* Cars have the disadvantage of costing a lot of money to repair. *e)* Cars have the advantage of speed. *f)* One of the advantages of having a car is that you don't have to depend on public transport.

D 1 *a)* Whereas fifty years ago families rented homes, nowadays the majority of families own their homes. *b)* Fifty years ago 5% of the population worked in agriculture, while nowadays only 3% work on the land. *c)* While fifty years ago only rich people had cars, nowadays many families own two cars. *d)* Whereas fifty years ago only a few people went abroad, nowadays millions of people go on holiday to Spain and Morocco. *e)* Fifty years ago children could leave school at fourteen, whereas nowadays children have to stay at school until they are sixteen. *f)* While fifty years ago people married in their late twenties, nowadays they marry in their early twenties or do not bother to get married at all.

E 1   *a)* buried in the country   *b)* within commuting distance of the large conurbations.
  2   *a)* Harold Magna is a freelance journalist working in London.   *b)* Harold lives in a new block of flats near Chelsea football stadium.   *c)* Harold once set his heart on a beautiful cottage built in 1792 near his parents' home.   *d)* The problem is that Harold has a lot of friends living in the centre of London.   *e)* Harold is considering the idea, suggested by his father, of renting a weekend cottage about 50 km from London.

UNIT 10

A 1   *a)* peak viewing hours   *b)* leisure time   *c)* prompted   *d)* boom   *e)* impact   *f)* advent   *g)* horizons   *h)* genius   *i)* lethargic
  2   *a)* F   *b)* F   *c)* F   *d)* F   *e)* F   *f)* F   *g)* T   *h)* F   *i)* F
  3   (suggested answers) *a)* According to Julia Elliott, most people spend their evenings watching television.   *b)* According to Julia Elliott, the effect of continual violence on television is that it loses its impact.   *c)* Television is giving people new interests, and these interests might stop people watching television.
  4   *a)* The average woman.   *b)* 'Their' refers to the vast majority of the population.   *c)* 'It' refers to the programme the speaker is asking about.   *d)* 'Them' refers to people in general.

C 1a   *a)* He will be feeling happy.   *b)* He probably won't be feeling sorry that he is leaving.   *c)* He may be reading a newspaper.   *d)* He is hardly likely to be drinking whisky.
  1c   *a)* His wife will be waiting for him.   *b)* He is bound to say thank you to the nurses.   *c)* He may well give a present to the Sister.   *d)* He may not be walking steadily.   *e)* His wife is unlikely to be feeling happy.   *f)* His wife is sure to start arguing with him again.   *g)* His wife is hardly likely to tell him about her boyfriend.   *h)* He may find out about her boyfriend.
  2a   *a)* In all probability fashions will be different.   *b)* There can be little likelihood of us driving the same types of car.   *c)* It is within the bounds of possibility that men will be living on Mars.   *d)* We are virtually certain to be arguing about the same things as we do now.   *e)* There is absolutely no chance that cities will look the same.
D 1   *a)* What   *b)* Which   *c)* What   *d)* Which   *e)* Which   *f)* What   *g)* What   *h)* Which   *i)* What   *j)* What

E 1   *a)* Whether people used to be happier in the past is difficult to judge.   *b)* That people did not have the same opportunities is quite obvious.   *c)* That the standard of living has risen is clear for all to see.   *d)* Whether people have benefited from technical progress seems questionable.

UNIT 11

A 1   *a)* laudable   *b)* deplorable   *c)* cut down on   *d)* discriminate   *e)* corrupt   *f)* assess   *g)* the media   *h)* motives   *i)* sympathise   *j)* take exception to   *k)* means   *l)* sketchy   *m)* implemented   *n)* eroded
  2   *a)* F   *b)* F   *c)* T   *d)* T   *e)* T   *f)* F   *g)* T   *h)* F   *i)* T   *j)* F

C 2a *a)* Only by closing down one school will the council be able to save money. *b)* The new bus timetable is intended to make the service more efficient. *c)* The main aim behind the proposal to build a new old people's home is to cater for the growing proportion of old people. *d)* The main reason for the company withdrawing this product from the market is to carry out further tests. *e)* Holding the meeting at 7.30 is intended to enable everyone to attend. *f)* Only by paying them the money you owe will you avoid prosecution. *g)* The main idea behind demolishing a lot of old buildings is to erect new office blocks.

D 1 *a)* He worked more hours than normal so as to earn enough money to go to America for a holiday. *b)* When he got to America he bought a car so that he would be able to come and go as he pleased. *c)* He drove very slowly so as not to have an accident. *d)* He bought a camera in order to have a permanent record of his holiday. *e)* When he got home he stayed away from work for a week so that he could have a rest after his exhausting holiday.

E 1 *a)* Had we known your phone number we could have contacted you. *b)* Should the T.V. repair man call today I can be contacted at this number. *c)* Had there not been a serious drought in parts of Africa recently, a lot of animals would not have died of thirst. *d)* Should the council approve the plan for a local arts centre it would be a great victory for the local arts campaign. *e)* Were there to be a total ban on nuclear weapons, millions of people would feel much safer. *f)* Were more money to be spent on universities, primary and secondary education would have to be cut. *g)* Should the level of unemployment increase further the trade unions will demand action from the government. *h)* Had Shakespeare not lived at the same time, Jonson would be more famous than he is. *i)* Should anything go wrong, let me know.

F 2 *a)* equality of opportunity *b)* treat women badly/like second class citizens *c)* unconventional beliefs, exploited *d)* are prejudiced *e)* discriminated against

RESOURCES FILE

Department of the Environment
ROAD TRAFFIC ACT 1972

Test Centre: BARTON

N 483557

Statement of Failure to Pass Test of Competence to Drive

Name MR J.D. GLEETHORPE

Address 5 LEACOCK ROAD, BARTON.

has this day been examined and has failed to pass the test of competence to drive prescribed for the purposes of section 85 of the Road Traffic Act 1972.

Charles Ray
Authorised by the Secretary of State to conduct tests.

Date 29.9.'76

Examiners have regard to the items listed below in deciding whether a candidate is competent to drive. The matters needing special attention are marked for your information and assistance and should be studied in detail.

See "Your Driving Test" (D.L. 68) Part II, paragraphs 1-21

1. ☐ (a) Oral test of knowledge of the Highway Code.   ☐ (b) Eyesight test.

SPECIMEN

These numbers refer to the rules in the HIGHWAY CODE
↓

CONTROL

2. ☐ Take suitable precautions before starting the engine;
3. ☒ Make proper use of/accelerator/clutch/foot brake/gears/hand brake/steering;
4. ☐ Move off smoothly/at an angle/on a gradient/on level/straight ahead;
5. ☐ Make normal progress to suit varying road and traffic conditions;
6. ☐ Stop vehicle in emergency/promptly and under control;
7. ☐ Stop machine in emergency/promptly and under control/making proper use of the front brake; | 28, 85
8. ☐ Reverse into a limited opening either to the right or left/under control/with reasonable accuracy/with proper observation; | 28
9. ☐ Turn round by means of forward and reverse gears/under control/with reasonable accuracy/with proper observation; | 28

ROAD PROCEDURE

10. ☐ Look round before moving off; | 30, 31, 56, 63, 78, 80
11. ☐ Make proper use of the mirror well before } signalling/changing direction/overtaking/ Take rear observation well before   } stopping; | 26
12. ☐ Give signals/correctly/in good time/by direction indicators/by arm; | 25, 27, 40, 50-59, 72, 74-78, 81, 97
13. ☐ Take correct and prompt action on all signals by/traffic signs/traffic controllers/take appropriate action on signals given by other road users; | 34
14. ☐ Exercise proper care in the use of speed; | 26, 31, 78, 80, 82
15. ☒ Act properly at cross roads/road junctions:— | 34, 70
   (i)   proper use of/mirror/signals/brakes/gears/when approaching; | 70
   (ii) correct regulation of speed when approaching; | 70-73, 76, 81
   (iii) looking right, left, and right again BEFORE emerging; | 55, 57, 59, 61, 78-80
   (iv) emerging with due regard for approaching traffic; | 82, 83
   (v)   correct positioning of vehicle { before/after turning right; { before/after turning left; | 78
   (vi) avoidance of cutting right-hand corners; | 31, 52-56, 58-60, 63-69, 78, 79
16. ☐ Overtake /meet/cross the path of/other vehicles safely; | 29
17. ☐ Keep well to the left in normal driving; | 38-41, 48, 80
18. ☐ Allow adequate clearance to/cyclists/pedestrians/stationary vehicles; | 42-47
19. ☐ Pedestrian Crossings/approach at a proper speed/stop when necessary/avoid overtaking at or approaching/avoid dangerous signals to pedestrians; | 97-99
20. ☐ Select safe position(s) for normal stop(s);
21. ☐ Show alertness and anticipation of the actions of/cyclists/pedestrians/drivers.

DRIVING EXAMINERS ARE NOT PERMITTED
TO DISCUSS DETAILS OF THE TEST.

GUIDANCE NOTES ARE CONTINUED
ON THE OTHER SIDE.

DL 24
(March 1974)

L.P. 56-1416 1/75

1 a) What happened during Mr Gleethorpe's test?
  b) How did Mr Gleethorpe feel about the examiner?
  c) Should the test be changed?
  d) What did Mr Gleethorpe have to do?

2 *a)* What was Charles' story when he arrived home?
   b) Describe Mary's attempts to visit Charles.
   c) Mr Smith's letter to Mary's bank manager.

```
 817413 POHDD G
TS 13/K LN

SMITH   5 GOLDEN SQUARE   BURLEY

CHARLES  ARRESTED  STOP  NO VISITS DESPITE REQUESTS  STOP

CONTACTED BRITISH CONSUL  STOP   MONEY NEEDED  FROM  MY  ACCOUNT  STOP

PLEASE  ARRANGE  STOP

        MARY
```

"*I think you'll be very happy with us.*"

B | Work

1 *a)* An advisable career?
  b) Professional army or conscript army?
  c) The navies of the future.

2 *a)* The characteristics of businessmen.

This Philips dictation machine could save you £4 an hour

£4 an hour. That's how much it can cost you all the time a secretary spends in your office, taking or waiting for dictation.

Install a Philips dictation machine, like this up-to-the-minute desk-top 97, and you release her from the time-consuming routine of notebook dictation. And start saving real money.

Check your own costs. And whether the answer comes out at £4 an hour, or more, or less, the saving you can make will add up to a lot of money in a year.

With a Philips dictation machine on your desk you save aggravation, as well as money. You can dictate exactly when it suits you, while the secretary gets on with other things that must be done. Equally, Philips dictation equipment is often the answer to making a shared-secretary arrangement work.

For details of the Philips 97, and all the dictation machines in Britain's best-selling range, just fill in and post this coupon to:

Philips Electrical Limited,
Business Equipment Division, Century House,
Shaftesbury Avenue, London WC2H 8AS.

Please send me
Full details of the Philips range of desk top and portable machines.

Name ....

Position ....

Company ....

Address ....

....

Postcode .... Tel: ....

ST22

PHILIPS   Simply years ahead.

---

3 *a)* Describe the job of i) a secretary
                                ii) a businessman.
   b) A secretary writes to Philips about this advertisement.

120

With hair meticulously rollered for a training session in the heat, a young member of Cuba's hurdling squad goes through her paces

Above: high-jumper Lucia Duquette (nearest camera) limbers up.

Southampton College of Art
Part-time Prospectus

c | Leisure time

1 *a)* How to become a top athlete.
 b) Government subsidies for sport?

2 *a)* Your idea of leisure?
 b) How can I escape boredom?

Pop Pollution

MICHAEL HEATH
reports yet another attack
on our beach heads

3 *a)* 'Our beaches have become intolerable', says town councillor.
 b) People at the seaside.

D | Social organisation

1 *a)* Describe the incident.
  b) Arrange a meeting to discuss the complaint.
  c) 'The end of prejudice? Hopes for the future.'

COMMISSION FOR RACIAL EQUALITY

Elliot House 10/12 Allington Street London SW1E 5EH

Application for assistance from the Commission in connection with a complaint or prospective complaint of unlawful discrimination under the Race Relations Act 1976.

CAN THE COMMISSION FOR RACIAL EQUALITY HELP?

Although individuals who allege that they have suffered racial discrimination have the right of bringing their own cases before the courts and Industrial Tribunals, they can also apply to the Commission for Racial Equality for assistance. The Act gives the Commission discretion to assist an individual who is an actual or prospective complainant, where the case raises a question of principle; where it is unreasonable, having regard to the complexity of the case or the position of the individual vis-a-vis the other party, to expect the individual to deal with the case unaided; or where some other special consideration applies. In such cases, the assistance which the Commission may afford includes giving advice, seeking a settlement, arranging for legal advice or assistance or representation. Legal costs incurred by the Commission will be charged to any costs (but not to any damages) payable to the complainant.

Where a person makes a written application for assistance, the Commission is required, within two months of receiving the application, to consider it, to decide whether or not to grant it, and to inform the applicant of its decision.

1

Please state your full name and address in BLOCK CAPITALS.

Name: __S. J. SINGH.__

Address: __3a DOVER TERRACE__
__LONDON S.E.22.__

Telephone No: Home _____   Work __01-621-7752__

2

How would you describe yourself in terms of colour, race, nationality or ethnic or national origin?

__INDIAN__

3

Whom are you complaining about?

Name and address of individual or organisation:
__'THE HEART OF OAK' PUBLIC HOUSE,__
__FOLKESTONE ROAD, LONDON S.E.22.__

Official position of person being complained against:

1

4 Please give as exactly as possible the time and date of the incident that you are complaining about.
If you believe racial discrimination against you is continuing, please say so.

Time: **DECEMBER 24th**   Date: **10.30 p.m.**

NOTE:

Protection against victimisation

"Please note that the Act contains provisions designed to protect from victimisation those who bring proceedings, or give evidence in connection with proceedings."

5 What are your reasons for believing that you suffered racial discrimination?
Describe as fully as you can what took place.

On 24th December my friend Gurmukh Singh and I visited The Heart of Oak Public House to have a quiet drink. We were neatly dressed and had not had any drinks before visiting the public house. I ordered a pint of mild for myself and a double whisky for my friend. The barmaid who I think was about 40 yrs old, five feet tall with dark hair and glasses, ignored us completely. Several white customers who came in after us were served without any difficulty. After waiting about 15 minutes I asked politely if I could see the manager. The barmaid continued to ignore me and I was forced to raise my voice to attract her attention. When I did so a man who appeared to be the manager came up to the counter, pointed his finger at me and said, "Right, that's it, out! Out! I won't have your kind in here". Not wishing to cause any trouble we left without any argument. I believe we were treated in this way because of our Indian origin. At no time were we impolite to him or the barmaid. I saw no black customers there

6 Please give name, address and telephone number of any witnesses to any part of what took place.

Name: **P.R. SINGH**   Name: **N.J. CRISP**

Address: **3a DOVER TERRACE**   Address: **52 FERRIS TERRACE,**
LONDON S.E.22   **LONDON S.E.22**

Telephone No: _____

7 Can you provide the names and addresses of anyone [in] similar circumstances?

NO

8 Have you applied for assistance elsewhere, e.g. Com[munity] Organisation, Citizens' Advice Bureau, etc? If so, pl[ease]

NO

9 If you are a member of a trade union, give its name.

—

10 Have you complained about this matter to an Industrial Tribunal or county court?

NO

11 I wish to apply for assistance under Section 66 of the Race Relations Act 1976.
I understand that the Commission has discretion in granting assistance and I will be informed within two months whether such assistance will be granted in my case, and if so what form it will take.

Signature: *S.J. Singh*   Date: **4th January**

Please send the form as soon as possible to:

The Complaints Officer
Commission for Racial Equality
Elliot House
10/12 Allington Street
London SW1E 5EH
Telephone: 01-828 7022

You will receive an acknowledgement to this application within the next few days.

If you have any difficulty please contact a complaints officer at the Commission.

Printed by Interlink Longraph Ltd.   4

123

2 a) Arrange a meeting between the council and representatives of interested groups to discuss spending on education.
b) The council's plans explained.

Where your money goes

	£m
EDUCATION	177
PLANNING AND TRANSPORTATION	28
POLICE	23
PUBLIC PROTECTION	10
SOCIAL SERVICES	23
RECREATION	5
OTHERS	11
Reserve for INFLATION	17
	£294m

EDUCATION

	£m
PRIMARY—149,820 pupils, 6,000 teachers, 621 schools	43
SECONDARY—111,610 pupils, 6,735 teachers, 113 schools and sixth form colleges	53
FURTHER—128,000 full-time and part-time students, 2,829 teachers, awards, and teacher training etc.	40
SPECIAL—5,606 pupils, 573 teachers	7
35½ million school meals and 12 million bottles of milk	15
Share of pooled education	9
Youth, careers, and support services	10
	£177m

PLANNING AND TRANSPORTATION

	£m
MAINTENANCE AND IMPROVEMENT OF ROADS AND BRIDGES 41 miles of motorway, 155 miles of trunk road, 4,921 miles of other roads	18.5
Bus and other transport subsidies	2.5
Design and support services	5
Planning services	1.5
Road safety, coastal protection, car parks etc.	.5
	£28m

POLICE

	£m
SALARIES AND PENSIONS 1 Chief and 4 Assistant Chief Constables 41 Chief Superintendents and Superintendents 185 Chief Inspectors and Inspectors 415 Sergeants 2,299 Constables 132 Cadets 132 Traffic Wardens 692 other personnel	18
Equipment, supplies and transport	2
Premises and other services	3
	£23m

This leaflet shows how the money is spent on these services, and how much of the average individual ratepayer's contribution is devoted to each service.

The figures only apply to the County Rate. You will, of course, be paying for District Council and Water Authority services in your total rate bill.

Average Ratepayer's contribution
£1·25 per week
...the price of 50 plain cigarettes

Average Ratepayer's contribution
18p per week
...the price of a small bottle of beer

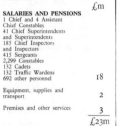

Average Ratepayer's contribution
7p per week
...the price of a small ice cream

PUBLIC PROTECTION

	£m
FIRE SERVICE 55 fire stations 151 fire engines and other vehicles 1,305 full-time and part-time firemen 167 other personnel	5·5
REFUSE DISPOSAL Incineration, tipping and pulverising (over ½ million tonnes)	2.5
Consumer protection, analyst service, registration, coroner's office, oil pollution, land drainage etc.	2
	£10m

SOCIAL SERVICES

	£m
CHILDREN—1,511 in residential care and 867 with foster parents, 76 children's homes	5
OLD PEOPLE—69 homes with places for 3,185 old people plus places for 368 in other homes	6.5
Other homes, hostels, special centres for disabled and mentally disordered	2.5
Day nurseries and other day care services	1
913 home helps aiding 10,600 people	2
538 social workers	2.5
Support services, 665,000 meals to elderly and housebound	3.5
	£23m

RECREATION

	£m
LIBRARIES—77 full-time and part-time, 19 million book issues	4
RECREATION—Grants, parks, archives and museum services	1
AND	£5m

OTHERS

	£m
Contributions to Capital expenditure	5.5
Magistrates' Courts and Probation Committees	2
Maintenance of buildings and other support services	1
Miscellaneous services	2.5
	£11m

INFLATION

	£m
The County Council has budgeted for inflation to average 11% during the coming financial year	£17m

Average Ratepayer's contribution
14p per week
...the price of a newspaper and a comic

For further information about the Hampshire County Council Budget for 1976-77 contact the County Treasurer's Department at The Castle, Winchester, telephone Winchester 4411.

Remember that you can pay your rates by instalments if you wish. Details are obtainable from the Treasurer of your District Council who will also be able to deal with any other queries you may have about your rates bill.

Average Ratepayer's contribution
7p per week
...the price of a small bar of chocolate

Average Ratepayer's contribution
18p per week
...the price of a large packet of sweets

Average Ratepayer's contribution
11p per week
...the price of two packets of crisps

1 *a)* How can people be so selfish?

b) 'A plan for the future: proposals for aid to developing countries.'

Last year hundreds of old people died of the cold.

It was a mild winter.

To be safe, old people must have a constant room temperature of above 60°F.

So please, visit the elderly regularly and make sure they're warm in winter.

The Health Education Council

2 *a)* Living on an old-age pension: a case study.
   b) The plight of the aged.
   c) The problems of having a granny in the family.

3 *a)* The difference between blind people and sighted people.

   b) Raising money for the blind.

4 *a)* Children with space to play: what advantages have they got?

   b) An architect defends the urban environment.

How well can your fingers read?

Not very well, we expect. But if you were blind, your fingers could be the key to normal living.

By using modern methods–including a computer–the RNIB has been able to provide more braille to meet the increasing demand.

However, braille instruction, literature and music represent only a part of a wide ranging service provided by the RNIB for Britain's 120,000 blind people.

Without your legacies and generous donations, we could not continue to maintain the help blind people need: Sunshine Nurseries and Schools for blind children, Talking Books, rehabilitation centres for the newly blind, homes and holiday hotels, training and employment schemes, research into blindness and over 300 aids for use in everyday life.

Why not turn a thought into a gift of money now.

RNIB
ROYAL NATIONAL INSTITUTE FOR THE BLIND
224 GREAT PORTLAND STREET LONDON WIN 6AA

Under the Finance Act 1975, bequests to charities up to a total of £100,000 are exempt from Capital Transfer Tax. Registered in accordance with the National Assistance Act 1948.

LIFESPAN

The sun is shining and school has broken up but there's no place to play in safety for these London children

Pressure for a place to play

F | Advertising

It does the job of an overnight soak, a dash of bleach or a good scrub in just 45 seconds.

FREND
SPRAY & WASH

breaks down stains
and grime in 45 seconds
ready for washing

Shifting most stains and grime used to need soaking, scrubbing, even bleaching.

Now, you can get the same result in just 45 seconds. Simply spray Frend onto everyday stains, even the most stubborn, and after 45 seconds pop the clothes into the wash.

Use Frend every washday for clean, stain-free laundry. The easy way.

FREND – THE 45 SECOND SOAK.

no more soaking
no scrubbing

1 *a)*   The power of advertising.

Slow-down. Speed-up. Stop-dead. By remote control.

FERGUSON
Videostar

There's never been a video recorder to offer you more.

All the advantages of a video recording system plus the capacity to slow down the picture, freeze it to a crisp, clear still, or speed it up to cover any ground you don't want to waste time on. And you can do it all in armchair comfort · with the Ferguson Videostar remote control.

The Ferguson Videostar deluxe is just what you've been waiting for. And it doesn't stop there. You can build a complete home video system with Ferguson – black and white or colour video cameras with sound, even a fully portable video recorder are all among the Ferguson Videostar range. And because they're Ferguson, you'll know they're the best.

Recording and playback of material may require consent
See Copyright Act 1956 and the Performers Protection Act 1958 22

FERGUSON
Technology you can trust

Ferguson Videostar Video Cameras

Ferguson Videostar Portable Recorder.

2 *a)*   Video equipment – its effect on modern living.

3 *a)* Would you like a credit card? Why? Why not?

"It doesn't matter if you're a party of four or forty, ring us with your name and American Express Card number, and the best available seats in the house are yours"

Tom Pate, Manager, National Theatre

The American Express Card says more about you than cash ever can. It is recognised and welcomed all over the world.

You can book your seats at the theatre by telephone and sign for bills at many fine stores, restaurants, hotels and car-hire companies. There is no pre-set limit to your spending – you set the pattern on spending limits with the Card as you use it. You can purchase tickets for a long-distance flight or a world cruise.

The enrolment fee is £10. Additionally, there is a subscription of £10, renewable each year. There are no automatic interest charges, but you are required to settle your accounts promptly on receipt.

Carry the Card and entertain in style.

"I strongly recommend you apply now"

129

4 *a)* Husbands or
washing-up machines?
b) Inside the house of the future.

G | Danger

1 *a)* Punishment and prevention.
b) You borrowed a car and
crashed it while under the
influence of alcohol.

CAMPAIGN FOR NUCLEAR DISARMAMENT (CND)

Affiliated to the International Confederation for Disarmament and Peace
United Nations Association, National Peace Council

Eastbourne House, Bullards Place, London E2 0PT   01-980 0937

Organising Secretary—Duncan Rees.

Dear Friend,

CND ANNUAL APPEAL - £3500 by CHRISTMAS

This is a very important time for those of us who are concerned about nuclear weapons and the threat they pose to peace. On the one hand we have the British Government boasting about the horrific nuclear weapons that we still have and pressing ahead with plans to maintain and develop new ones — on the other hand CND in its work has made some important advances. However, in order to make these advances irrepressible, we still have much work to do.

CND has been active throughout the year, and especially after major events we have been increasing our membership noticeably. There have been several important events for CND during the year, including our labour movement conference and the Easter demonstration and — one of the most important of all — our forthcoming programme on BBC2 (details elsewhere).

The prospects for CND expanding, and indeed the vital need for us to do so, are therefore immediate. However, we urgently need finances — not just to keep going, but to gain in strength. If we are to increase our influence, and avoid having to curtail our activities due to lack of money, then *we must have £3500 by Christmas 1976.*

CND plans to be working more effectively and with more support by the end of the year — but to be able to do this we are depending on YOU responding generously to this appeal.

We have just passed the 31st anniversary of the Hiroshima and Nagasaki bombings — and that, plus our forthcoming TV programme, is maintaining and even extending interest in CND. However, we must commit ourselves not just to maintaining CND, but also to advancing it substantially: the need is great, the time is right. Please help us now in this appeal and get us moving even more quickly towards nuclear disarmament.

Yours sincerely,

Duncan Rees
Organising Secretary.

Alistair Macdonald
Treasurer.

2 *a)* The best ways to raise money.
  b) Answer an invitation to a fund-raising meeting.

131

"Grandma, can I have $ 20?"

She's got a problem. At 16 years old. She needs the money to support her drug habit. As she grows older she'll need more and more and she won't be able to get it legally.

If uncured, she'll turn to crime. Or prostitution. Or both.

That's the way it goes, these days. Drugs, a kick, a habit – then descent into the ugly world of crime and drug dependence. It starts early. Statistics show your child may encounter his first pusher when he's about 16 years old.

16 years old! Not your child? Not in your area? Don't you believe it. At 16, children, see others using drugs. They try them. And that's just how it starts. Unless you do something about it now.

Contribute to the United Nations Fund for Drug Abuse Control. A world-wide effort to clean up a world-wide problem.

It takes an organization like the U.N. to wage the battle effectively. In the rich cities where drugs are used and in the poor areas where they are grown. (And in between where they are traded.) It's an international problem that is difficult to fight only on a national basis. It takes the U.N.

And it takes money. Money to help countries train police and custom officers to control drug traffic. Money to compile world-wide experience on drug abuse education and prevention methods. Money to study the social cause of drug abuse. Money to educate farmers to grow a cash crop other than the opium poppy. And on and on.

You can help. Send the U.N. some of that needed money. Help launch a programme that is aimed at protecting your children from the terrible effects of drugs. Please do it now. There isn't much time.

Attach your cheque to the coupon.

United Nations Fund
for Drug Abuse Control
c/o United Nations
Palais des Nations
1211 Geneva 10
Switzerland

Name

Address

Amount of contribution

3 *a)* Should drug-users be punished?
b) The results of drug-taking: a vicious circle.

4 *a)* Obligations in a consumer society. New laws to reduce waste and pollution.

Do you want a cigarette more than you want your baby?

When a pregnant woman smokes she puts her unborn baby's life at risk. Every time she inhales, she poisons her baby's bloodstream with nicotine and carbon monoxide.

Smoking can restrict your baby's growth inside the womb. It can make him underdeveloped and underweight at birth.

It can even kill him.

In just one year, in Britain alone, over 1,500 babies might not have died if their mothers had given up smoking when they were pregnant.

If you give up smoking when you're pregnant your baby will be as healthy as if you'd never smoked.

The Health Education Council

5 *a)* More than £5m is spent on ciagarette advertising: less than £½m is spent on anti-smoking advertisements.

133

ACKNOWLEDGEMENTS

We are grateful to the following for permission to reproduce copyright photographs:
All-Sport Photographic Ltd., for page 121; Alan Band Associates for pages 79 & 89; Barnaby's Picture Library for pages 19(bottom) & 83; Sunday Times for pages 127 & 133.

We are also grateful to the following for permission to reproduce copyright material:
Author's Agent for the lyrics of *Simple Twist of Fate* by Bob Dylan
Copyright 1974 by Ram's Horn Music, P.O. Box 289, Cooper Station, New York 10003. Rights for U.K. and Republic of Ireland controlled by Big Ben Music Ltd., The Music Centre, Engineers Way, Wembley, Middx; The Anti-vivisection League for page 29; Mick Davis for page 69; Controller of Her Majesty's Stationery Office for page 118; Royal Navy (Officer Entry Section) for page 119 (bottom, left); Punch Publications (Michael Heath) for pages 119 (middle) and page 121 (bottom); Southampton College of Art for page 121 (top, right); Commission for Racial Equality for pages 122 & 123; Hampshire County Council for page 124; Oxfam for page 125; Health Education Council, London, for pages 126 & 133 (bottom); Royal National Institute for the Blind for page 127 (top); Southern Evening Echo for page 128 (top); Borough of Newport (Civic Centre) for page 128 (middle); JVC (U.K.) Ltd., for page 128 (bottom); American Express Company for page 129; David Williams and Ketchum Ltd., for page 130 (top); The Royal Society for the Prevention of Accidents for page 130 (bottom); Campaign for Nuclear Disarmament (CND) for page 131; United Nations Office at Geneva for page 132; Philips Electrical Ltd., for page 120.